Elementary Android App Development

Elementary Android App Development

Victor Kaiser-Pendergrast

Please send comments on this book to:
v.kaiser.pendergrast@gmail.com

ISBN: 1481931350   REV: Fin_rev_a

EAN-13: 978-1481931359

Table of Contents

About the Author

Victor Kaiser-Pendergrast graduated from Pope John XXIII Regional High School in Sparta, New Jersey. He is studying computer science in Rutgers University's Honors Program. He started developing for Android when it was first released in 2008. Android development became one of his hobbies, and he began creating various applications for his own personal use.

In 2012, he released his first applications to the market, and, spurred by positive feedback, he began to become more deeply involved in writing apps for Android to solve problems and inefficiencies he faced. In the first few days of 2013, he released BadgIn Attendance Tracker, a fully featured attendance taking app. In all, his apps are downloaded thousands of times each month, currently with over 150,000 users.

In September 2012, he began an independent study in Android development; this book is the product of that study.

Preface

Audience
This book is intended for those wishing to begin developing Android applications, with little or no prior experience with Android. It is assumed that readers have an amount of Java knowledge that roughly equates to taking an introductory course in Java.

Motivation
This book seeks to make learning Android development available to students and hobbyists by consolidating and curating the plethora of information available into one book aimed at those new to the Android platform.

How to use this book
In order to get the most out of this book, it is necessary to follow the examples and try them for oneself. This cannot be more highly recommended. Furthermore, after trying the code snippets provided by this book, experiment with the code by adding code or by making changes.

   The source code of all of the major example applications is available at *https://code.google.com/p/elementary-android-dev-projects/*

Acknowledgement
This book was inspired by my high school computer science teacher, Mrs. Elizabeth Buniak. Without her, I would never have written this. I would also like to thank my father, Mr. J. Stephen Pendergrast for letting me use his HTC G1, which first sparked my interest in Android.

1 Java Review

1.1 Introduction

This book assumes that you have already learned Java, whether from an instructor or on their own. Nevertheless, it is necessary to have a strong command of the language. This does not mean that you have to know all the standard Java classes, but what is required is knowledge of Java syntax, how Java works in general, how to use packages and a few key classes, and object oriented programming.

1.2 Common Classes

The following is a brief overview of some common Java classes and their methods that are needed for Android development. Just about every standard Java class may be used in an Android application, so bear in mind that the following list is only a

2   ELEMENTARY ANDROID APP DEVELOPMENT

quick reference of what will be most important. For example, a developer might use the *Math* class often, but generally might only use *DatagramPacket* in applications involving networking. Reflection will not be used in this course, as there is no real use for them other than debugging and inspection of other's classes.

- **ArrayList**: In Android, *ArrayList* (and sub-classes of *List)* will be used quite often, so be familiar with the constructor and methods like add, get, replace, remove, and, insert.
- **Math**: The math class will be used for common math operations like *sin, cos, tan, sqrt,* and *pow,* as well as high accuracy mathematical constants like π and e, and a way to retrieve pseudo-random numbers with the random method.
- **InputStream**: *InputStream* and its subclasses like *BufferedInputStream* will be used for file input or receiving network packets.
- **OutputStream**: Like *InputStream,* but used to send instead of receive.
- **Map**: The implementations of *Map,* like *HashMap,* will be used to facilitate the creation of simple databases and is similar to an Android specific class called *Bundle* that will be used often.

These few classes are critical to understand when beginning Android development. The majority of classes used in Android apps (especially more basic apps) are Android specific. The Java Swing classes will not be used when designing interfaces on mobile phones, but knowing Swing may help in understanding the hierarchy of an interface.

The classes listed above will be the most critical to the projects outlined in this book. Knowing more classes will be beneficial of course, but remember that documentation exists so that it is not necessary to memorize every class.

1.2.1 ArrayList

All programming languages support arrays, which are fixed length lists that can contain a specific data type. In most languages, arrays cannot be resized, exceptions to this include fairly uncommon languages like D. Java has this implementation of an array with static size, but fortunately, it also includes a class called *ArrayList* which can dynamically change size.

In Java, an *ArrayList* can only contain objects. This means that by default, when getting values from *ArrayList,* the objects returned will be of the class *Object* and have to be cast to whatever class needed for use. The return class of ArrayList can be changed using generics; section 1.2.1.1 shows how to do so.

Because *ArrayLists* can only hold objects, no primitives are allowed. Therefore, if a program had to add *int* values to an ArrayList, they would first have to be made into *Integer* objects. This is done automatically at runtime, but when retrieving the value back from the ArrayList keep in mind that you will have to cast to *Integer*, not int.

This concept is demonstrated here:

```
ArrayList array = new ArrayList();
   int intValue = 4;
   array.add(intValue);

   Integer objValue = (Integer)array.get(0);
   if( objValue.intValue() == 4 ){
      //Do something here        when the value
      //of the Integer in the array is equivalent
      //of int 4
   }
```

Also note that when comparing the *Integer* to an *int,* you will have to use the *intValue()* method to get an *int* to compare to another *int*.

1.2.1.1   Generics

Generics are commonly used in Java, especially with abstract data types like collections.

Generics are used to remove the need to type cast for accessing methods and variables of objects in abstract data types as well as classes designed to be extended, such as *AsyncTask*. It is likely that an introductory Java course or book has taught generics, even if the term has not been mentioned. Generics are perhaps best understood by example.

Here is a snippet of code with an ArrayList without a generic:

```
ArrayList arr = new ArrayList();
   arr.add("This example does not use generics");
   String index0 = (String)(arr.get(0));
```

Notice that the object returned by arr.get(o) must be cast to a String before it is assigned to indexo.

Here is the same functionality achieved by declaring the generic object type for ArrayList as String.

```
    ArrayList<String> arr = new ArrayList<String>();
    arr.add("This example does use generics");
    String index0 = arr.get(0);
```

In this example, the generic Object contained by ArrayList has been changed to String, so now there is no need to cast because *arr.get(o)* will automatically return a String.

Generics are extremely useful and are used to great extent in abstract data types like ArrayList and Map. Note that generics were only introduced in Java 5, so some legacy versions of Java do not support them. This will not be an issue on Android, as Java 6 is required.

1.2.2 Math

Anyone who has coded in Java should be familiar with the Math class. Every language has its own equivalent. In Java, Math provides the means to do square roots, exponents, trigonometry, logarithms, and can find the minimum and maximum of two values, can generate random numbers, convert between radians and degrees, as well as perform other tasks. Here are some examples.

```
    double squareRootOfFour = Math.sqrt(4);
    double exponent = Math.pow(3, 4); //3 to the 4th power.

    double sin45Degrees = Math.sin( Math.toRadians(45) );
    //trig methods take radians, toRadians and toDegrees
    //can be used to convert between radians and degrees
    sin45Degrees = Math.sin( Math.PI/4 );
    //Math contains the constants pi and e

    double log = Math.log(7);
    int min = Math.min(4, 7); //min is 4
    int max = Math.min(4, 7); //max is 7
```

1.2.3 InputStream

InputStream may be unfamiliar to many students starting to learn Java, however, it is extremely important in software design because it allows the reading of files and packets that come from the network or the internet.

The example below uses *InputStream* to read from a file:

```
    File myFile = new File("C:/exampleText.txt");

      //Create a new InputStream that reads from myFile
FileInputStream inputStream = new FileInputStream(myFile);

      String text = "";
      int nextChar = inputStream.read();
      while(nextChar != -1){ //Read until the end of the file
         text += (char)nextChar;
      }
    //Always close an InputStream after it is done being used
      inputStream.close();

      System.out.println(text);
```

In this case, the subclass of *InputStream, FileInputStream*, is being used. *FileInputStream* accepts a Java *File* object in its constructor, which points to the location of the file on the operating system's file system.

As can be seen, calling read() on an *InputStream* returns an *int*. The *int* represents a *byte* and has value from 0-255. At this point, you may be asking why a whole *int* (four *bytes*) is being used for just one *byte*, the answer is that at the end of the input (in this case the end of the file), read() will return a -1. Calling read(byte[]) will put data into the byte array supplied and will read as many bytes as the array is long. This is more useful when dealing with data of a known length, otherwise, use read() to go byte by byte.

The above code shows how to deal with the end of the input with a while loop, and will read until it hits the end of the file. After the program is done reading, the *InputStream* must be closed if it will not be used later; closing releases any system resources used.

This example shows using *InputStream* with a file, but it is also very common to read network packets with *InputStream*, which is something that will be explored later.

1.2.4 **OutputStream**

Like *InputStream, OutputStream* has largely the same purpose, except it writes rather than reads. *OutputStream* is often used for file output and the sending of network packets.

```
    File myFile = new File("C:/exampleText.txt");
      FileOutputStream outputStream = new FileOutputStream(myFile);
```

```
byte[] text = new String("This text will be written").getBytes();

outputStream.write(text);

//Always close an OutputStream after it is done being used
   outputStream.close();
```

As you can see, an *OutputStream* can write byte arrays or individual bytes in a way similar to how *InputStream* can read one or multiple bytes. Also, do not forget to close an OutputStream, or the operating system will keep resources in use. Many operating systems disallow a single file being edited by two different programs at the same time. You may have encountered messages to the extent of "This file is currently in use," in the past during general computer use because a file was still being used by a program. Calling close() will release control of the file and allow other programs to use it.

1.2.5 **Map**

In Java, the *Map* class is the simplest way to implement a basic database. Other means to create databases, like SQL offer more flexibility, but require more setup. Simply put, a Map registers an ID (often referred to as the *key*) with a value. By using generics, the key and value can be objects of any class. Pay special attention to the fact that Map cannot have two identical keys.

Here is an example of creating a simple Map and getting some of its values. Note that this example uses *HashMap*, which keeps its keys and values in no specific order.

```
HashMap<Integer,String> map = new HashMap<Integer,String>();
   map.put(1, "one");
   map.put(2, "two");
   map.put(3, "three");

   String text = "Numbers: " + map.get(1) +
                        ", " + map.get(2) +
                        ", " + map.get(3);

   System.out.println(text);
```

This example simply adds three key and value pairs to a *HashMap* by using the put(key,value) method and then shows how to get values from their respective keys. map.get(1) will return *"one"* because *"one"* is the value associated with the key 1.

Maps also remove key and value pairs by calling remove.

```
map.remove(2);
```

Remove accepts a key and will remove the key and its associated value.

The *Map* class is used often for the creation of simple databases. Also, a class specific to Android called *Bundle* is used to send and receive data between screens of an app's interface and between applications.

1.3   Extending Classes and Implementing Interfaces

Perhaps the most significant unique aspect of Java is that it is Object Oriented. Classes can extend other classes and automatically contain all the methods and variables of the parent. In Android, there will be many times when it is necessary to extend or implement a class or interface.

To extend a class, simply declare your class, like so:

```
class MyClass extends ParentClass {
   @Override
   public void parentClassMethod(){
      super.parentClassMethod();
      //add extra functionality here
   }
}
```

MyClass is what is being written and *ParentClass* contains methods and variables *MyClass* will inherit. Any protected or public methods in *ParentClass* can be overridden or added to in *MyClass*. In this case, the method *parentClassMethod* in *ParentClass* is being overridden. The base functionality from *ParentClass* is still there because of the call *super.parentClassMethod* is made, but extra functionality is added afterwards.

Interfaces are simply lists of methods that another class implementing them must define functionality for. Interfaces are used throughout Java. Examine the *List* interface, which is implemented by *ArrayList*, *LinkedList*, and *Stack*. Interfaces allow developers to create different classes with methods that serve the same purpose, but do so in different ways.

```
public interface Fish {
   public void eat();
   public void  move();
   public void update();
}
```

Here is an example: say that you are writing a simulation of a fish tank. *Fish* might be an interface with the methods eat, move, and update. Multiple different kinds of fish now would be separate classes that implement *Fish*. Some fish might be carnivores, so their eat method might involve hunting other fish, while other fish might seek out plants or krill in their eat methods. The update method might define the behavior of the individual species of fish, so that would be different for every class of fish, but every fish has an update method.

Interfaces offer an easy way to create general categories of classes and access them. Referring back to the fish tank example, what would be an easy way to update all the fish? The simplest way to do this would be to store all the current fish in an *ArrayList* that holds object type *<Fish>* by using generics. Then use an iterator or a for-each loop to call *update()* on every fish in the list. Interfaces are an extremely powerful tool that are used often in practice.

In order to use the *Fish* interface, simply declare a class as implementing *Fish*.

```
public class Shark implements Fish{

   @Override
   public void eat() {
      //add hunting behavior here
   }

   @Override
   public void move() {
      //swimming logic goes in here
   }

   @Override
   public void update() {
      //decide between
```

```
      //eating and moving
   }
}
```

As can be seen, implementing an interface is relatively easy. Simply declare the same methods as in the interface and write the code for them. Now you can have all different kinds of *Fish* with different behaviors share the same parent class and therefore can be treated similarly. Here is an example of how an *ArrayList* of all different kinds of *Fish* could have all the *Fish* be updated.

```
ArrayList<Fish> fishList = new ArrayList<Fish>();

//add a lot of different fish here
for(Fish a : fishList){
   a.update();
}
```

Using interfaces allows similar classes with the same methods to be treated as if they were all members of one class. Interfaces are extremely powerful tools and will be used throughout this text.

Every application written in this book will have at least one case where one class extends another, so understanding how this works is critical.

2.3.1 @Override

In the first example of *MyClass* extending *ParentClass*, note the @Override flag that precedes the definition of *parentClassMethod*. This tells the compiler that the following method is being overridden.

Overriding a method without *@Override* will work, however, if you do use *@Override* and try to override a method that does not exist in the parent class, the compiler will throw an error, which will alert that method name may be spelled differently or does not exist in the parent class.

Using *@Override* is a good habit because the compiler will throw an error if the method to be extended is not spelled correctly or has different arguments, which can save a lot of time when initially debugging applications.

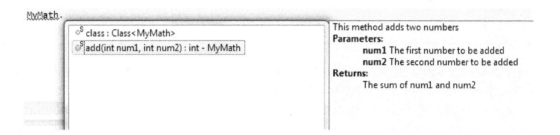

1.4   Understanding Javadoc

Javadoc will be used heavily in samples in this book, and it is highly recommended that you use it as well. Documenting code will drastically speed up development time on all but the most basic projects you write.

Writing Javadoc is easy, immediately preceding a method or class, start Javadoc with /**, notice that this is exactly like a block comment, but with an extra asterisk. To end Javadoc use */ in exactly the same way as if one was ending a block comment. In Eclipse, typing /** before a method and pressing **enter** on the keyboard will immediately fill in everything you can define. Here is an example:

```
/**
 * This method adds two numbers
 * @param num1 The first number to be added
 * @param num2 The second number to be added
 * @return The sum of num1 and num2
 */
public int add(int num1, int num2){
    return num1+num2;
}
```

The parameters for the method and the return type all can be documented, as well as a general comment for the method.

In Eclipse pressing **ctrl** and **space** at the same time will bring up an autocomplete pop-up. After typing any part of a class's name or a method, opening auto complete will show all possible classes and methods that begin with those characters.

For methods, in addition to showing the method name and arguments, auto complete also shows that method's associated Javadoc in an easy to read format:

This method adds two numbers

Parameters:

> **num1** The first number to be added

> **num2** The second number to be added

Returns:

> The sum of num1 and num2

Fortunately for developers, all the Android specific classes and methods have Javadoc written for them, so it is easy to learn new methods on the fly. On larger projects in this book that involve many classes spread across multiple files, writing Javadoc will be essential for programming efficiency.

Thanks to Javadoc, most of the time it is unnecessary to have the entire Android documentation open to find method names and the arguments they take. The example below shows a common scenario. In this case, a developer forgot exactly which method he or she should use to display a *Dialog* named *alert*. By opening the auto-complete pop-up, the Javadoc descriptions for every method and public variable can be examined.

2 Development Tools

2.1   Setting up the Environment

In this course, we will be developing Android applications which are written in Java. To do this, will we need to use the Eclipse IDE (Integrated Development Environment). Other IDEs are supported (like NetBeans for example), but not nearly to the extent of Eclipse, which is recommended by Google (the developers of Android) and is their officially supported tool.

Note that the setup procedure may change with future updates. The following dialogs and menus that the following explanation refers to may be different now from when this book was written. If this is the case, use the instructions provided on *http://developer.android.com/sdk/index.html*

Eclipse and Android are both written in Java, so we will need to download and install the latest Java Development Kit (JDK). If you are on Mac 10.6 or higher, you already have a JDK. For those on Windows and Linux, the JDK can be found on Oracle's website at www.oracle.com/technetwork/java/javase/downloads which is most likely the first result on any search engine for the search "jdk". At this point in time, the Android Development Tools require JDK 6. Download the installer specifically for your operating system. Keep in mind that if you are on a 32-bit operating system, you must get the 32-bit installer. If you are unsure if your computer is 32-bit or 64-bit, download the 32-bit installer. Follow the specific instructions for your operating system. If you are on Windows, simply run the .exe file. Other operating systems may require more work (Linux will require the creation of an environment variable, that will not be covered here, as it may change with new releases of JDK. Easy to follow guides may be found by searching the internet).

Once the JDK is installed, we need to download Eclipse, which can be found on www.eclipse.org/downloads. It is recommended that you use Eclipse Classic. The Android Development Tools are version independent of Eclipse; this book will be using Eclipse Classic 4.2. Like with the JDK, choose 32 or 64-bit. If you chose the 32-bit JDK you **must** use a 32-bit version of Eclipse, and likewise with 64-bit. Eclipse is easy to install, simply download the appropriate compressed archive and extract it to someplace easy to remember like the desktop or in your user folder.

Now open the extracted Eclipse folder. If you are using Linux or Unix, make sure that Eclipse.sh has the runnable permission. Usually this is done by right clicking it, selecting properties, and checking a check box named something to the extent of "Mark as executable". Eclipse.sh or Eclipse.exe will be what you will open to launch the IDE, so you may want to create a shortcut or alias to it for easier access.

Upon opening Eclipse, it will ask where you want your workspace to be. This is where all of your Eclipse preferences and projects will be. The default is fine, but you can change the path of it if you'd like. Press **Okay** to dismiss the dialog and continue the launching of Eclipse.

At this point, you need to install the Android Development Tools plugin for Eclipse. This can be done by selecting **Help**, and then **Install New Software**. This will open a new window. In the upper right, click the **Add** button. In the **Name** field type ADT, and in the **Location** field enter the following url: https://dl-ssl.google.com/android/eclipse/

Close this dialog by clicking **OK**. Now check the checkbox next to **Developer Tools** and click **Next**. Here you are shown the tools that will be downloaded, click **Next**. Accept the license agreements and finally click **Finish**. At this point, you may see a security warning, click OK. Eclipse will ask to restart when the installation is finished.

Upon restarting and after you chose your workspace, the ADT plugin will prompt you to either set the path to an already downloaded Android SDK or download a new copy of it. We haven't previously downloaded the SDK, so allow it to download it. You may be prompted to restart Eclipse again.

Now open the Android SDK Manager (a button located in the toolbar directly to the right of the save and print buttons). Check the documentation, SDK platform, and ARM system image and click *Install*. Accept the license agreements. Once the installation completes, restart Eclipse.

▲ ☐ 🗔 Android 4.2.2 (API 17)			
☑ 📄 Documentation for Android SDK	17	2	🖴 Installed
☑ 📱 SDK Platform	17	2	🖴 Installed
☐ 🧪 *Samples for SDK*	17	1	⬇ *Not installed*
☑ 📱 ARM EABI v7a System Image	17	2	🖴 Installed
☐ 📱 *Intel x86 Atom System Image*	17	1	⬇ *Not installed*
☐ 📱 *MIPS System Image*	17	1	⬇ *Not installed*
☐ 🏭 *Google APIs*	17	2	⬇ *Not installed*
☐ 📄 *Sources for Android SDK*	17	1	⬇ *Not installed*

This concludes the setup for our development environment.

If you plan on developing on a physical device, there is another step or two you will need to take, but if you plan on only using the emulator, you may skip to the end of this section. On your Android device, if you are running Android 3.0 or higher, go to Settings, then Developer Options, then finally check "USB Debugging". On older versions of Android, this option is located in Settings, then Applications, then Developer Options.

If you using a Linux or Mac computer, everything will work at this point. On Windows however, some Android devices may require drivers, which will usually be found on the device's manufacturer's website. An easy way to find it is to perform a Google search for "ADB Driver for " and the name of your device.

Congratulations! At this point you now have the bulk of the tools used to develop professional quality mobile applications!

2.2   Creating a New Android Project

The process of creating a new Android project in Eclipse has been facilitated by the plugin we installed earlier. In Eclipse, simply go to File, then New, then Other. From here find the *Android* folder, expand it and chose *Android Application Project*.

The next screen will ask you to give a project name, primary Java package, Build SDK, and Minimum SDK. An appropriate name would be something like "First Project". The defaults for everything else will be fine.

After that, you will be taken to an icon generator page. In this simple example, this will not matter, but later on, when publishing to the market, a clear, good looking icon is crucial.

The next dialog box that shows up asks if you would like to create a main activity and if it should be blank or contain a two layer navigation (Master Detail Flow). For the sake of simplicity, chose **BlankActivity** which does not contain much pre-written code, other than a blank definition of the *MainActivity* and a screen that displays "Hello world!"

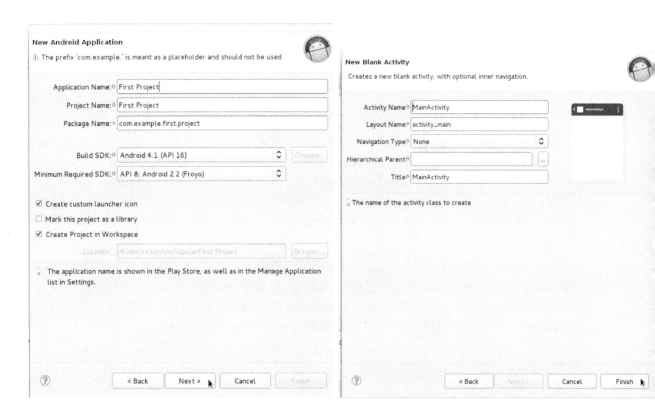

The next step asks you to name the activity and choose if you would like it to use a template for inner navigation (like tabs or a drop-down menu system). In this first example, make sure **Navigation Type** is set to be none, and leave everything else default.

That is all there is to creating a new project! Currently this blank application will only bring a user to a page with "Hello world!" written on it, which makes it a good starting point and template to develop further.

If you would like to run this application, either plug in a device which you have setup in Section 2.1, or you may use the emulator. Press the green run arrow in Eclipse located on the top toolbar. If you have properly set up a device, a dialog will be shown asking to select it. Upon choosing your device, the project will be uploaded and automatically run on your device.

If you will be using the emulator, but have not created a virtual device, the ADT will ask to create a new one.

The dialog box below shows how to create a new virtual device. Simply give it a name, select what version of Android it should run (preferably the latest version, in this case 4.2), choose how large of a virtual SD Card to make (in MB). The SD Card does not have to be very large, bear in mind that a 1024 MB virtual SD Card will take up a whole gigabyte on your computer's hard drive. SD Card file operations will not be covered until later, and a virtual device can be edited at any time, so it is best that the SD Card size be made a small size for now, like 12 MB.

Using **Built-in** gives a choice of preset screen resolutions of common devices, and **Resolution** allows to manually set a screen resolution. Although modern day phones have resolutions of 720 x 1280 and higher, emulators with that high resolution will run very slowly unless you are on a fast computer. For the best performance on lower end hardware, choose QVGA. For most computers, use WVGA.

It is recommended that you enable **Snapshot**, which will save your emulator's state when you close it, so next time it is opened, it will not have to boot and will be ready in seconds.

Now when you run a project, the emulator will start (if it is not already running), and the application will be uploaded and opened. Note that start-up times of the emulator may be long, so be sure to use **Snapshot**.

Click **Create AVD** and you will have a virtual device to develop on. At any time, you may edit the AVD you created and change any of its characteristics you set up.

2.3 Overview of Eclipse

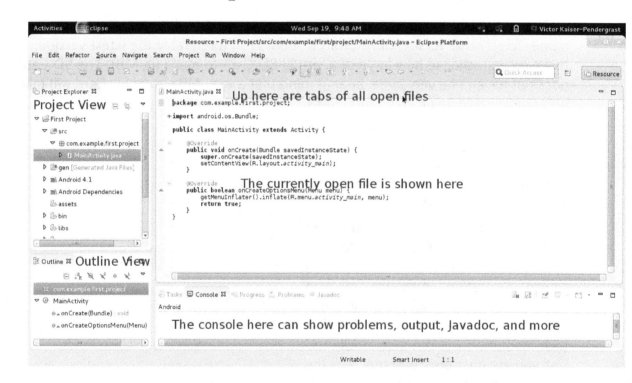

Above is a quick overview of Eclipse with the First Project that has been created.

On the left is the Project View which will show all open projects. Projects can be explored in a way similar to how file managers work on any operating system. The small triangles next to folders can be clicked to expand them.

Open First Project and navigate to MainActivity.java as shown in the picture. Double clicking on a file will open it, try it on MainActivity.java and the large source window to the right will show the contents of the file.

Above the source window is a space for tabs of all currently open files. Right now there is only one open, but in the future, when working with multiple files, these tabs will make switching among them easier.

Above the tabs of the Project View is the primary toolbar. Buttons on there include the green run arrow, debugging, and more. Towards the left are two buttons that have been added by the Android Development Tools. The first shows the Android mascot in a box with a down arrow. This will take you to the Android SDK Manager which will allow you to download new versions of the SDK as they are released. Adjacent to the right of that is a button that looks like the Android mascot on the screen of a device. This opens the Android Virtual Device Manager, which is where you may have already created a new virtual device.

Below the Project View is an outline. The outline will show all defined methods of the file being worked in. Most people do not find it entirely useful, so you may want to press the minimize button on it (the dash) and allow more space for the Project View.

The Console will be of great use. Like the Source View, it also has tabs that switch between multiple views. The Console tab will show output of programs, Progress shows a progress bar when building a program or saving, Problems will show any syntax or compiler errors, and Javadoc shows the Javadoc for the currently selected method.

2.4   Using Logcat

You may be familiar with writing Java applications in which *System.out.print* would allow the printing of a string to the console for debugging purposes. That exact method will not work in Android, but fortunately a tool called Logcat has the same functionality and more.

Logcat will show up as a tab in the Console area of Eclipse. By default, it may not appear. If this is the case, simply navigate to **Window** then **Show View**. This will open another selection choice; choose **Other**. Expand the **Android** folder and select **Logcat**.

By now, in Eclipse's Console area, the Logcat tab should have appeared. Debugging to Logcat is simple, but will be covered later after the basics are covered.

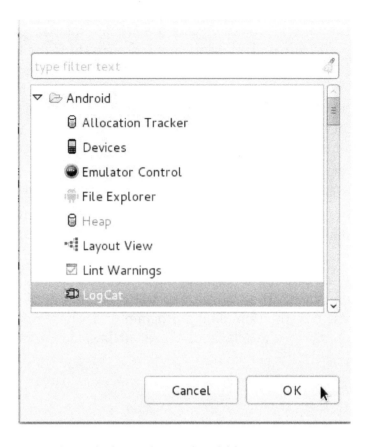

At this point, every tool needed in Eclipse should be set up.

2.5   Example Source Code

The source code of all of the major example applications is available at *https://code.google.com/p/elementary-android-dev-projects/*

This is no substitution for working through the examples given and explained in this book, but the code available online will let you get example programs running quickly.

3 Android Basics

3.1 Core Components

There are a few core parts of every Android application. Activities run the actual Java code and logic of the app. The layouts (what is shown on the screen) are defined separately from the Activities. Activities can decide what layout to show at a given time. In general, an Activity corresponds to a single layout and declares what to run on different inputs in the layout (like buttons and checkboxes) and/or what to do when sensor values change (like the GPS). All Activities must be defined in the Manifest, which can also add certain characteristics per Activity.

3.2 The Manifest

In a way similar to how other applications are written, every Android application requires a Manifest which defines every Activity. If an Activity is not defined in the Manifest but there is a call to launch it, the application will immediately throw a *ClassNotFoundException* and crash.

In addition to simply defining Activities, the Manifest holds the application name, version, and icon, as well as asks for Permissions from the operating system. Permissions are used to request additional features of a device's hardware (such as the camera or GPS) or access to personal information and services (contact information, the ability to make telephone calls or send text messages).

When installing an application, the user will be notified as to what Permissions are being asked for. This is done primarily for security. If a user is about to install notepad application and sees that it asks for access to the contact list and internet access without good reason, he or she might think that the application is malicious. Because of this, it is always best to ask for as few Permissions as possible.

Open the manifest of First Project now. It is located in the First Project folder in the Project Explorer near the bottom and is called **AndroidManifest.xml**. You may be brought to a graphical layout with input boxes labeled **Package, Version Code,** and **Version Number**. If this is the case, on the bottom of the source view will be a set of tabs with labels like **Manifest, Application, Permissions, Instrumentation**, and **AndroidManifest.xml**. Choose **AndroidManifest.xml**, which will take you to the actual XML code instead of the graphical editor.

The graphical editors the ADT includes for XML files tend to make them seem more complicated than they are. The XML code view should look like this:

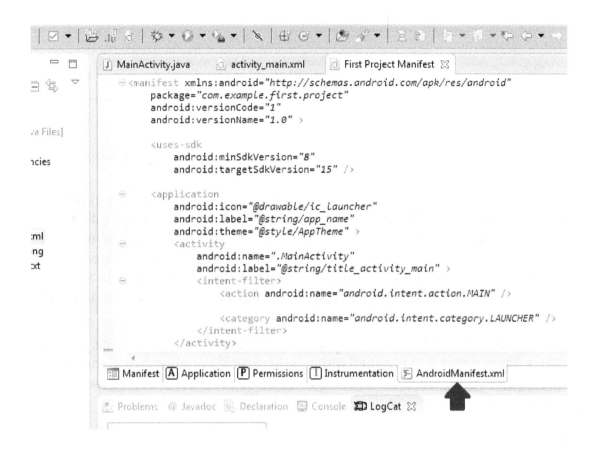

```
<manifest
    xmlns:android="http://schemas.android.com/apk/res/android"
    package="com.example.first.project"
    android:versionCode="1"
    android:versionName="1.0" >

    <uses-sdk
        android:minSdkVersion="8"
        android:targetSdkVersion="15" />

    <application
        android:icon="@drawable/ic_launcher"
        android:label="@string/app_name"
        android:theme="@style/AppTheme" >

        <activity
            android:name=".MainActivity"
            android:label="@string/title_activity_main" >
            <intent-filter>
                <action android:name="android.intent.action.MAIN" />
                <category android:name="android.intent.category.LAUNCHER" />
            </intent-filter>
        </activity>
```

```
    </application>
</manifest>
```

At this point, you may not be familiar with XML. Fortunately, XML is easy to learn and is very similar to design languages like HTML.

In XML, to make a node, < > are used. The first node (and the highest in the hierarchy of nodes) is called the root node. In the manifest, the root node is called *manifest*. Characteristics of each node are specified within the < >. In XML, all the nodes are organized in a tree fashion (similar to the way a computer's file system works; one could make the analogy that putting a node within another node is similar to putting a file in a folder, but the comparison is not quite exact), where nodes can branch off of other nodes.

manifest defines the *android* tag, *package*, *versionCode*, and *versionName*. If a node contains nodes within it, it is ended with >, otherwise if a node stands alone with no nodes inside, it is ended with />. In order to end nodes ended with >, use </*type*> where *type* is the kind of node.

```
<item1
    <!-- Add characteristics here -->
    <!-- This node will have no children,
         so it ends with />              -->
/>


<item2
    <!-- Add characteristics here -->
    <!-- This node has children, so
         the definition of manifest ends
         with >                          -->
>
        <node/>
        <node/>
        <node/>

</item2>
```

Note that manifest also contains the following line:

```
xmlns:android="http://schemas.android.com/apk/res/android"
```

This line must be the first characteristic in the root node in the manifest, because it defines the *android* tag that is used throughout the file. Now the keyword *android* can be used to refer to the link above anywhere in the file. The tag *android* is used in every node in the manifest and layout design.

In manifests, the *manifest* node is the root node and contains all other nodes, so it is ended at the very bottom of the file with </manifest>.

Inside the manifest node (underneath manifest in the hierarchy) are two more nodes – *uses-sdk* and *application*. The *uses-sdk* node is quite simple. All it defines are the version of Android to build for, and the minimum version of Android this application may be installed on. Android versions are given numbers, which can be found online on developer.android.com with the rest of the Android reference materials.

In this case, the minimum version number of Android is 8, which is version 2.3.3, Gingerbread, and the application is being built for version 16, Android 4.1, Jelly Bean. It is always recommended that the application is built for the newest version of Android. A list of the API version numbers relating to the more familiar Android version numbers is available on the developer website and can be found by searching "Android API Level List".

The other node underneath *manifest* is *application*. In *application*, there are a few characteristics are defined. The first is the icon to use for the app. You may notice that the icon is referred to as *@drawable/id_launcher*, this will be explained later with the way the resources work. Likewise with the label, which is the way the application's name shows, which is also located in *@string/app_name*. Finally, the application style is defined. Styles are used to change the appearance of application elements, usually for branding. For example, some applications change the color of buttons, the background, and text boxes to match the color of their icons or company logos.

The only nodes underneath *application* are the Activities. As mentioned earlier, every Activity has to be defined here. The *name* characteristic is the path of the Java class from the *package* defined in the root node, *manifest*. In this case, it is simply the Java class name preceded by a period because the Java class is at the top of the *package* defined in the manifest. This results in ".*MainActivity*", which in this case will be the Java class *com.example.first.project.MainActivity*.

Finally, some Activities have an *intent-filter* which will tell the system when to launch it. In this case, this Activity can be opened from the launcher (home screen). The *intent-filter* can also be used to have certain activities respond to a user opening specific file types or extensions, or on other actions, like if the device is put into a dock or if the camera button is pressed.

That is all there is for the Android Manifest. There is a lot of data compacted into this one file, but thanks to XML, it is not terribly difficult to decipher.

3.3   Project Directories

The files for any Android project are organized into two categories: source and resources. Source is the Java code that will run the application, whereas resources include everything else, such as pictures, layouts, sounds, and raw files.

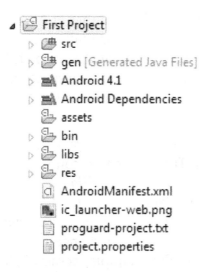

The **src** folder contains all Java packages and classes.

The folder **res** contains all resources. The resources are organized into several folders under **res**, some of which may or may not exist. At this point, only the most critical will be examined.

drawable contains all pictures for the app, whether they be icons, backgrounds, or anything else. You may notice there are many folders that begin with "drawable", like **drawable-hdpi**, **drawable-mdpi**, and **drawable-ldpi**. These are for specifying different icons for use with different screen densities. Usually for an application to be released, icons are scaled to different sizes for each screen density. The system automatically will scale the icons to appropriate sizes, but defining icons per screen density will speed up loading times by eliminating the scaling calculation and by creating icons for every density, a developer can make sure that there are no artifacts caused by the software scaling.

layout contains all the definitions of screen layouts. Screen layouts are written in XML and specify user interface elements, declare where they are located, determine what size they are, and set their characteristics. In a way similar to *drawable*, *layout* can also have multiple folders beginning with *layout*, the difference being that the alternate folders do not specify layouts for different screen densities, but rather different screen sizes. For example, on a large screen (like on a tablet), it might make more sense for an application to separate individual screens out into multiple panes. Consider an application that on a small screen (on a phone) has a screen of a list of subjects and upon selecting a subject shows another screen with details for that subject. On a tablet, it makes more sense to have a pane on the left side with the subjects and another pane on the right that shows the details on selection. Designs like this are facilitated by Fragments in Android, but that will be gone into more detail when layouts are thoroughly discussed.

values contains definitions for Strings, styles, and even primitive lists. It is recommended that text used in the user interface is defined in *values*, because it facilitates changing wording in the interface. Perhaps more importantly, *values*, in a similar way to *drawable* and *layout*, can have specific versions for different languages. If a developer has put his/her user interface text into values, he or she can simply add more translations into more specific *values* folders and the system will automatically use the correct language on whatever device it is installed on. As for styles, they let designers define customized versions of buttons and system attributes and apply them per user element, per screen, or globally over the entire application. Not only can there be specific *values* for different languages, but also for the version of Android being run. This is helpful to ensure that an application's style will look good on any version of Android. With Android 3.0, Google introduced the Holo style, which is highly recommended for use. Unfortunately, Holo is not available on devices before Android 3.0, so by using styles specified for lower versions of Android, developers can create fallback themes that keep the application's appearance mostly consistent across the older versions of Android.

menu contains definitions of what to fill the ActionBar with (on older devices, it fills the pop up that opens when pressing the menu button). Menu items have an order (based on the priority characteristic), text label, ID used for event listeners, usually an icon, and whether or not to show the icon in the ActionBar (always, never, or if there is room left).

The ActionBar:

The ActionBar is at the top or bottom of the application and contains main functionality of the application. Items that do not fit into the main part of the ActionBar (where the search icon is) will be automatically put into the Overflow menu (three vertical squares).[1]

Here is the overflow menu
opened after being tapped:

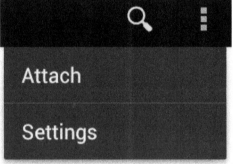

On older devices (before Android 3.0, which was released in spring of 2011), the same options populate the menu, which can be opened by pressing the menu button as shown below.

---

[1]   Note that on Android devices running Android 3.0+ and also have a physical menu button, the overflow menu button (three dots) will be hidden. Rather on these few devices, the overflow menu is opened by pressing the physical menu button.

3.4 XML Layouts

Like the Android Manifest, layouts are also written in XML. The hierarchical structure makes designing layouts mostly straightforward, although beginners may run into some struggles at first.

The best way to understand a layout is to see examples of how the various elements are used. Layouts are located under *res* and then *layout*. In First Project, the sole layout is named *activity_main.xml*. Like with the manifest, you may be brought to a graphical editor.

The layout graphical editor tends to make a mess of all but the simplest layouts, so it is imperative that layouts are designed in code. However, the graphical editor is still extremely useful when designing layouts, because it shows how the layout code will be rendered in real time. This means that whenever you are designing a layout, simply clicking the tab *Graphical Layout* will show how the layout will look.

Click the *activity_main.xml* tab on the bottom to see the code. It should look like this:

```
<RelativeLayout xmlns:android="http://schemas.android.com/apk/res/android"
    xmlns:tools="http://schemas.android.com/tools"
    android:layout_width="match_parent"
    android:layout_height="match_parent" >
    <TextView
        android:layout_width="wrap_content"
        android:layout_height="wrap_content"
        android:layout_centerHorizontal="true"
        android:layout_centerVertical="true"
        android:text="@string/hello_world"
        tools:context=".MainActivity" />
</RelativeLayout>
```

Similar to the manifest, the root node contains the definition of the *android* tag first.

It also defines the tag *tools*, which is used for debugging purposes.

The first characteristic defined is *android:layout_width*. This characteristic can take many values. Dimensions can be defined in raw pixels (example: 54px), in density independent units (example: 30dp), or with relative values (examples: match_parent, fill_parent, and wrap_content).

It is highly recommended that nothing be defined in raw pixels, because different screens have different densities of pixels. This means that text set with a height of 15px might look fine on some devices, but on others will be too small and unreadable.

Density independent units scale with screen size and density. Theoretically, 20dp will be the same size on any screen size and any screen resolution. Density independent units are generally used to create spaces or padding between buttons, or create margins. User interface elements (like buttons, textboxes, and icons) should not have dimensions in Density independent units, but rather should use *match_parent*, *fill_parent,* and *wrap_content.*

match_parent is the size of the node that contains the current node. In this example, the TextView will match the width of the RelativeLayout. The RelativeLayout is the root node in this case. *match_parent* for the root node will fill the screen.

wrap_content will make a view be only as big as necessary to hold what is contained in it. For example, using wrap content on this TextView will make the width only as wide as the text "Hello World" and only as tall as the single line of text.

fill_parent allows multiple views to fill a space, but it can be tricky for new developers to understand, so it will not be covered until layouts are gone through in detail in Chapter 6.

The next two characteristics, *centerHorizontal* and *centerVertical* do exactly as it would seem; they center the text in the middle of the RelativeLayout.

The *text* characteristic sets what text to actually display. *text* can either be set to a **literal** ("Hello World") or reference to a resource (as is the case in this example). It is recommended that nothing be defined as a literal for a few reasons. Primarily because multiple interface elements may have the same text and using literals would require the text to be changed in many places at a time if one wants to change the text.

Here is an example: a developer wants to change his "Settings" screen to be called "Preferences". If he had used literals, he would have to change title of the button that links to the "Settings" screen and he would have to change the page title of the "Settings" screen to "Preferences". This may seem like an exaggerated example, but when designing applications, scenarios like this do occur, especially towards the end of development when everything is being polished. Also, as mentioned earlier, the **values** folder can have more specific sets of values for different languages, so no extra code has to be written to set user interface elements to the device's native language

The text resource used in the TextView is defined in the **values** folder under **res**, which will be shown soon.

tools:context is solely used for the graphical view and will not affect the way the view is rendered in the emulator or on a device. Ignore it for now.

3.4.1 Experimentation

The best way to learn is through doing, so try experimenting.

At this point, try changing the RelativeLayout to LinearLayout, observe what happens in the Graphical View or on a device. Note that the TextView is not centered anymore. This is because LinearLayout does not support centering.

Try adding another TextView after the one already defined and define its text as a literal[2]. Also note that this new TextView is not underneath the other, but rather to the right. This is because by default LinearLayouts are oriented horizontally rather than vertically. This can be switched by setting the *android:orientation* characteristic to "vertical".

Also, try adding some more characteristics either of the TextViews. Remember that in Eclipse, pressing **ctrl** and **space** at the same time will open the auto-complete menu. At this point, you probably will not understand how to set most of these characteristics, but try adding *android:textSize* or *android:textStyle* (bold, italic, or bolditalic).

Open **values** under **res**. Now open **strings.xml**. Try changing the values of some of the strings contained in there. Remember that the original TextView referred to @string/hello_world. Note what happens to the layout.

3.5 Java Code

XML Layouts are great for defining the user interface, but without the underlying Java, no code will be run. The Java source can be found in the packages in the **src**

---

[2] Using literals is not good practice for production, but when first learning, there is no harm in them. On anything more complicated than simple Hello World type projects, only use references.

folder. In this case, the package is *com.example.first.project*, which was defined when this project was created.

The Activity launched when this application is first created is appropriately named **MainActivity**. Open it.

```
public class MainActivity extends Activity {

  @Override
    public void onCreate(Bundle savedInstanceState) {
        super.onCreate(savedInstanceState);
        setContentView(R.layout.activity_main);
    }

    @Override
    public boolean onCreateOptionsMenu(Menu menu) {
        getMenuInflater().inflate(R.menu.activity_main, menu);
        return true;
    }
}
```

Here you can see the source. Even though this app has no functionality, you can see that there still has to be code to set what layout to show and what buttons to put into the Action Bar or Menu. Note that this class extends **Activity**. Every application will have at least one Activity. Simply put, Activities manage the user interface by accepting input or making changes to it.

There are a few key methods in **Activity** that can be overridden.

3.5.1 onCreate

First of all, every **Activity** written for an app will have to override the method *onCreate*. It is easiest to think of *onCreate* as the constructor for the Activity. All the setup code will be written in *onCreate*. Because this class extends **Activity**, a call to the super class must be made. The method *setContentView* sets what layout is displayed. Right now, this project has nothing else to setup in the interface, so there is nothing else to be seen.

3.5.2 onCreateOptionsMenu

Like *onCreate*, *onCreateOptionsMenu* performs setup. However in this case, the only setup is telling the system what options to put in the action bar or options menu.

The menu is defined in an XML resource as can be shown here. In this case, it refers to the resource under *res* in the *menu* folder, and is called *activity_main.xml*.

3.5.3 onKeyDown

onKeydown is called whenever a key is pressed, whether it be on a physical keyboard, mouse, or joystick. *onKeydown* can also receive presses of the back, search, camera shutter, and volume buttons.

3.5.4 onKeyUp

onKeyUp functions exactly the same as *onKeyDown*, except it reports when keys are released.

3.5.5 onTouch

onTouch allows an application to intercept presses of the touchscreen. *onTouch* is especially helpful when designing games where non-standard user interfaces (that do not use pre-defined interface elements like Button) exist. *onTouch* can provide information about multiple touches of the screen at the same time, such as X and Y positions (measured in pixels of the screen), when touches begin or end, and the size of a touch, among other characteristics of each touch.

3.5.6 Other Methods

There are plenty of other methods that can be overridden, mostly dealing with the application lifestyle. With simple applications like this first project they are not necessary, but certainly with more complicated applications it will be necessary to save the application's state and free memory when the application is left or closed.

4 XML Layouts

4.1 Introduction

The previous chapter outlined some basic XML syntax when explaining the manifest and the basic Hello World layout. This chapter will serve to further explain hierarchy in XML and go into depth on how to piece together user interfaces that look clean and are easy to navigate. The subsection of XML needed is not terribly difficult to learn, and those with HTML experience will find XML familiar.

4.2 Hierarchy

XML is a hierarchy of nodes. Each node is below another (with the exception of the root node). You should be familiar with the manifest, as it was discussed in the prior chapter. For reference, here is the manifest code for the First Project application.

```
<manifest xmlns:android="http://schemas.android.com/apk/res/android"
    package="com.example.first.project"
    android:versionCode="1"
    android:versionName="1.0" >

    <uses-sdk
        android:minSdkVersion="8"
        android:targetSdkVersion="15" />

    <application
        android:icon="@drawable/ic_launcher"
        android:label="@string/app_name"
        android:theme="@style/AppTheme" >

        <activity
            android:name=".MainActivity"
            android:label="@string/title_activity_main" >
            <intent-filter>
                <action android:name="android.intent.action.MAIN" />
                <category android:name="android.intent.category.LAUNCHER" />
            </intent-filter>
        </activity>
    </application>
</manifest>
```

This simple flow chart shows the hierarchy of the manifest. At the top, the root node is appropriately called *manifest*. Immediately below it are *uses-sdk* and *application*. This can be seen from the code rather easily by the indentations.

Also note how *uses-sdk* is closed with "/>". Nodes without any other nodes underneath them can be closed this way as opposed to "</uses-sdk>". The latter will work just as well, but "/>" is a convenient short-hand.

Note how *activity* contains characteristics within its definition before the ">" and how its child *intent-filter* comes after. Pay attention to the closing of *activity* after the definition of its child *intent-filter* and *intent-filter*'s children. Finally, at the very end *manifest* must be closed.

If you are more comfortable with Java code, imagine

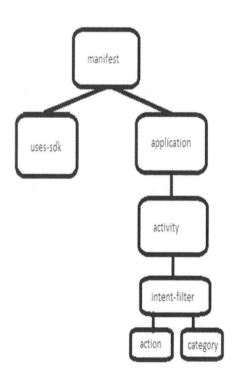

that each node is a set of braces like "{ }". Now just as with Java code, each brace must have a matching opposite brace, and each brace must eventually be closed.

For the purposes of writing Android applications, this is basically all the XML needed to know. Writing layouts for Android in XML is mostly about understanding how the Android layout renderer works and how views interact with each other.

4.3 Layout

In general, the highest on the hierarchy will be a layout. A layout is almost always the root node. Layouts render multiple children in a specific way. Examples include *LinearLayout* which renders its children linearly (like in a list) either horizontally or vertically one after another in the order defined.

Another common layout is *RelativeLayout*, which is what First Project originally used. *RelativeLayout* functions completely differently. It allows its children to align themselves with one another. For example, one can align with the bottom edge of the screen, or the right edge of another child. Relative layout also allows children to be centered in the screen.

4.4 General Practice

When writing interfaces, every view and layout **must** have the following two characteristics defined: *android:layout_width* and *android:layout_height*. Without these two characteristics set, the Android layout renderer will not know how large to make the views or layouts, and the application will immediately crash at runtime.

Also, you will see the characteristic *android:id* for almost every layout and view. *android:id* gives the view or layout a name so that the view or layout can be accessed later. This is especially important when writing the Java code, as the id will be used to get the state of views, and when using the *RelativeLayout*.

When defining an id for a view or layout, the syntax is as follows.

```
android:id="@+id/text1"
```

The @ is used to tell the system that this refers to a resource. You may have noticed that earlier when referring to string resources the example had *@string/hello_world*. @ can also refer to drawables, raw files, layouts, and more.

Because this ID has not been defined before, the syntax is @+. The + tells the compiler that if the id has not already been defined then define it now. In essence, this small snippet of code is creating an id called *"text1"* and then setting this view's or layout's ID to that. Also, a note on valid IDs, accepted practice is all lowercase letters with underscores separating words. Be sure that no ID has any spaces, as this would cause errors.

4.5 View

Views are the actual elements of the interface. Buttons, checkboxes, text input boxes, images, and more are all views. Shown below are in depth guides to every commonly used view.

4.5.1 TextView

TextView was used in First Project. A *TextView* simply displays text.

```
<TextView
        android:layout_width="wrap_content"
        android:layout_height="wrap_content"
        android:text="@string/hello_world" />
```

4.5.2 Button

Buttons are one of the simplest views. Buttons have a text label and can be pressed. To capture button presses, an *OnClickListener* has to be made, which will be shown later.

```
<Button
        android:layout_width="wrap_content"
        android:layout_height="wrap_content"
  android:text="@string/hello_world" />
```

Hello world!

4.5.3 ImageView

An *ImageView* simply shows an image.

```
<ImageView
        android:layout_width="wrap_content"
        android:layout_height="wrap_content"
        android:src="@drawable/my_image"
        android:contentDescription="@string/hello_world" />
```

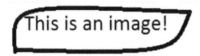

ImageView has a few unique characteristics. The first, *src* is the image to be displayed. *contentDescription* is used for accessibility purposes. If a visually impaired user wants to use your app, he or she can use a screen reader to assist in navigation. Usually this simply warrants reading the text of a view, but with *ImageView*, a screen reader will read the content description out loud.

4.5.4 ImageButton

An ImageButton is a button that has a picture instead of text.

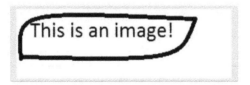

4.5.5 CheckBox

Checkboxes are very similar to Buttons, but they can be checked and unchecked instead of only pressed.

```
<CheckBox
        android:layout_width="wrap_content"
        android:layout_height="wrap_content"
        android:text="@string/hello_world"
        android:checked="false" />
```

Hello world!

Note that Checkboxes have one more characteristic than buttons called *checked* that allows the checkbox to be pre-set to be checked or not.

4.5.6 EditText

An *EditText* view allows a user to input text.

```
<EditText
        android:layout_width="wrap_content"
        android:layout_height="wrap_content"
        android:hint="@string/hello_world" />
```

No text, hint is visible:

Hello world!

User starts typing,

hint disappears:

a

The *hint* characteristic is the text to be shown in the edit text box when the user has not entered anything. Setting the *text* characteristic will fill the textbox with the supplied text. This is generally undesirable because a user trying to enter something into the textbox will have to first delete everything currently in it. The only exception to this rule is if the application has a default or saved value that populates the text input box.

The top picture shows the *EditText* with the hint, whereas the lower picture shows the textbox after one letter has been entered. Note that the hint text disappears without being explicitly deleted by the user.

4.5.7 **More Complicated Views**

There are other views that can contain views inside of them and specially arrange them or add some functionality. A common example is *ScrollView* which will let all of its children be scrolled if they go beyond the end of the screen.

Other views format their children in interesting ways, for example, *GridView* will put its children in a grid that can dynamically change the number of rows and columns based on available space. These views are more complicated to use and require something called an *Adapter* which is written in Java. These views are used in almost all interesting applications, but for the time being it is more important to become acquainted with the basics of the Android layout.

4.6   **Using RelativeLayout and LinearLayout**

RelativeLayout and *LinearLayout* are the two most common layouts. *RelativeLayout* specifically is an extremely powerful layout because it allows views and layouts to be positioned relative to other views and layouts.

4.6.1 **LinearLayout**

LinearLayout is the simplest of all layouts. All it does is put its children in vertical rows or horizontal columns in the order that the children are declared in the XML. There is only one unique characteristic to *LinearLayout*, which is *android:orientation*. Accepted values for *orientation* are *"horizontal"* and *"vertical"* which are rather self-explanatory as to their functionality.

```xml
<?xml version="1.0" encoding="utf-8"?>
<LinearLayout xmlns:android="http://schemas.android.com/apk/res/android"
    xmlns:tools="http://schemas.android.com/tools"
    android:layout_width="match_parent"
    android:layout_height="match_parent"
    android:orientation="vertical" >

    <TextView
        android:layout_width="wrap_content"
        android:layout_height="wrap_content"
        android:id="@+id/text1"
        android:text="First row" />

    <Button
        android:layout_width="wrap_content"
        android:layout_height="wrap_content"
        android:id="@+id/button1"
        android:text="Button in the second row"/>

    <TextView
        android:layout_width="wrap_content"
        android:layout_height="wrap_content"
        android:id="@+id/text2"
        android:text="Third row" />

</LinearLayout>
```

This simple example features a vertically oriented *LinearLayout* with three children, a *TextView, Button,* and then another *TextView*. For sake of understanding, each of the children has text identifying what position it is located in.

First row

Button in the second row

Third row

4.6.2 **RelativeLayout**

RelativeLayout is slightly more complicated to use than *LinearLayout*, but is far more powerful for designers. Instead of rendering its children in a list one after another, a *RelativeLayout* allows its children to be defined in relation to one another. This means that a button can be declared to be underneath a *TextView* or to the left of a *CheckBox*. *RelativeLayout* also allows views or other layouts to be centered horizontally or vertically in its parent, or aligned with any side of the screen.

```xml
<?xml version="1.0" encoding="utf-8"?>
<RelativeLayout xmlns:android="http://schemas.android.com/apk/res/android"
    xmlns:tools="http://schemas.android.com/tools"
    android:layout_width="match_parent"
    android:layout_height="match_parent"
    android:orientation="vertical" >

    <CheckBox
        android:layout_width="wrap_content"
        android:layout_height="wrap_content"
        android:id="@+id/check1"
        android:text="check1: aligned with the top"
        android:layout_alignParentTop="true"
        />

    <CheckBox
        android:layout_width="wrap_content"
        android:layout_height="wrap_content"
        android:id="@+id/check2"
        android:text="check2: underneath check1"
        android:layout_below="@id/check1"
        />


    <Button
        android:layout_width="wrap_content"
        android:layout_height="wrap_content"
        android:id="@+id/button1"
        android:text="button1: right of check1"
        android:layout_toRightOf="@+id/check1"/>

    <TextView
        android:layout_width="wrap_content"
        android:layout_height="wrap_content"
        android:id="@+id/text1"
        android:text="text1: aligned with bottom and centered horizontally"
        android:layout_alignParentBottom="true"
        android:layout_centerHorizontal="true"/>
```

```
</RelativeLayout>
```

As you can see, children of a *RelativeLayout* inherit characteristics such dealing with relative positioning, centering, and aligning with the parent. The following table has all the characteristics that children of a *RelativeLayout* receive.

Characteristic	Function
layout_centerHorizontal, layout_centerHorizontal	Centers the view horizontally or vertically. Can be set to *true* or *false*.
layout_toRightOf, layout_toLeftOf, layout_below, layout_above	Puts the view to the right, left, below, or above the view with the ID supplied.
Layout_alignParentTop, layout_alignParentBottom, layout_alignParentRight, layout_alignParentLeft	Makes the view flush with the specified side of the parent layout.
layout_alignRight, layout_alignLeft, layout_alignTop, layout_alignBottom	Aligns the specified side of the view with the view of the ID supplied. Aligning the bottoms of two views will make their bottom edges flush with each other on the same level.

The result of the above code produces a screen that looks as follows. The text descriptions given to the views explain what characteristics are used on each. If *RelativeLayout* still seems confusing, try playing around with the code above. By experimenting with the XML and seeing how it affects the graphical view, you will gain an intuitive understanding of the workings of *RelativeLayout*.

☐   check1: aligned with the top   button1: right of check1

☐   check2: underneath check1

text1: aligned with bottom and centered horizontally

4.7   Compounding Layouts

When creating an interface, note that layouts can contain not only views, but also other layouts. For example, if you wanted a horizontal row of buttons in a vertically oriented linear layout, you could put a horizontal *LinearLayout* in the vertical *LinearLayout*.

☐   check1: aligned with the top   button1: right of check1

☐   check2: underneath check1

```xml
<?xml version="1.0" encoding="utf-8"?>
<LinearLayout xmlns:android="http://schemas.android.com/apk/res/android"
    xmlns:tools="http://schemas.android.com/tools"
    android:layout_width="match_parent"
    android:layout_height="match_parent"
    android:orientation="vertical" >

    <TextView
        android:layout_width="wrap_content"
        android:layout_height="wrap_content"
        android:text="First row" />

    <LinearLayout
        android:layout_width="match_parent"
        android:layout_height="wrap_content"
        android:orientation="horizontal" >

        <TextView
            android:layout_width="wrap_content"
            android:layout_height="wrap_content"
            android:text="Row 2 Linear Layout" />

        <Button
            android:layout_width="wrap_content"
            android:layout_height="wrap_content"
            android:text="Button 1" />

        <Button
            android:layout_width="wrap_content"
            android:layout_height="wrap_content"
            android:text="Button 2" />
    </LinearLayout>

    <TextView
        android:layout_width="wrap_content"
        android:layout_height="wrap_content"
        android:text="Third row" />

</LinearLayout>
```

This code's root node is a linear layout with three direct children: a *TextView*, a *LinearLayout*, and then another *TextView*. The first time seeing this code might be puzzling, but seeing how it is rendered may help:

The following diagram shows how the layouts are rendered in depth. The entire bounding box is representative of the *LinearLayout*. The blue lines between the three rows show how this *LinearLayout* is vertically stacking its children. Meanwhile, the middle element is another *LinearLayout*, although this time it is horizontally oriented, and it is represented by the red box.

Hopefully, this diagram offers some insight as to how layouts can be nested inside each other to create more interesting and useful designs.

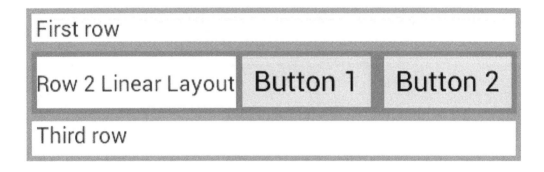

In this example, the same functionality could have been achieved with a single *RelativeLayout*, but the code would have been much less readable. Furthermore, layouts as children of other layouts will become especially important and common as interfaces designed in this course become more complex.

4.8 Weights

Up to this point, it may have seemed that all layouts would have to have a pre-defined size (which is usually a bad idea, because the layouts will not scale nicely), wrap their content, or take up the size of their parents. Sometimes, it might make more sense for one layout to occupy two-thirds of a screen, and another layout to occupy the remaining third. The characteristic *layout_weight* can give layouts and views this functionality and will prove to be a very powerful tool.

Note that *layout_weight* on will only work on a layout or view if that layout or view is inside of a *LinearLayout*. *layout_weight* takes a float or an integer as its argument, but for the sake of simplicity and readability, it is better to only use integers. Each layout in the parent *LinearLayout* is given a weight (with some exceptions that lead to interesting functionality, as shown later).

The size of a view or layout is equal to its weight divided by all the weights in the *LinearLayout* parent. For example, if there is a *LinearLayout* with two buttons in it, one with weight 1 and one with weight 2, the first one will occupy $\frac{1}{1+2}$ of the space, or $\frac{1}{3}$ of the space. Likewise, the other button will occupy the other $\frac{2}{3}$ of the space.

The code for rendering the above two buttons follows:

```
<?xml version="1.0" encoding="utf-8"?>
<LinearLayout xmlns:android="http://schemas.android.com/apk/res/android"
    android:layout_width="match_parent"
    android:layout_height="match_parent"
    android:orientation="vertical" >
```

```
    <Button
        android:layout_width="match_parent"
        android:layout_height="0dp"
        android:layout_weight="2" />

    <Button
        android:layout_width="match_parent"
        android:layout_height="0dp"
        android:layout_weight="1" />

</LinearLayout>
```

Note that in that code, the characteristic *layout_height* on the buttons is set to odp, but the buttons are still rendered. *layout_weight* will always take precedence over setting dimensions manually. Although usually discouraged, in this case setting *layout_height* to a constant is a good thing. When using weights it is highly recommended to use constants for dimensions, because *match_parent* or *wrap_content* will perform lookups and calculations that will not be used anyway. Some may dismiss this as a micro-optimization and therefore not important, but the performance loss from many small discrepancies can increase initial rendering speed of a layout.

Weights are very effective at designing layouts with different panes, which are especially used on tablets and other large screen devices. For example, a designer might want to have a list occupying the left quarter of the screen, and a details page showing more information about items selected in the list. In this case, the list pane can have a weight of 1, and the details pane could have a weight of 3.

4.8.1 Combining Weights with Pre-defined Sizes

Views with weights can be combined with other views that do not have a weight, but rather pre-defined sizes like *wrap_content* or *match_parent*. In this case, the weight does not correspond to the percentage of the total space that the view will occupy, but rather will be the percentage of the space remaining after adding all the views with hard coded sizes.

This leads to interesting and useful functionality. Perhaps in an instant messaging application, there is a layout with a *Button* labeled "Send" and an *EditText* to input the message. The *Button* will have a width of *wrap_content*, but the *EditText* has to scale to fill the

rest of the screen width. Using a weight on the *EditText* and on nothing else will fill the screen as shown below.

```xml
<?xml version="1.0" encoding="utf-8"?>
<LinearLayout xmlns:android="http://schemas.android.com/apk/res/android"
    android:layout_width="match_parent"
    android:layout_height="match_parent"
    android:orientation="horizontal" >

    <EditText
        android:layout_width="0dp"
        android:layout_height="wrap_content"
        android:layout_weight="1"
        android:hint="@string/input_message" />

    <Button
        android:layout_width="wrap_content"
        android:layout_height="wrap_content"
        android:text="@string/send" />

</LinearLayout>
```

Weights offer an easy way to make interfaces that scale with the screen size. Unlike other platforms, Android devices have screens of different resolutions, sizes, and aspect ratios, but declaring layouts properly and using techniques like weights will make variations in displays a non-issue.

4.9 Efficiency

On mobile platforms designing for efficiency is crucial. Modern processors for mobile devices are exponentially faster than the processors from just a couple years ago, but doing things efficiently is still important. Even the slightest delays are very jarring for users and adversely affect their experiences with an app. Most performance issues originate with poorly designed Java code or long operations running on the interface thread, but the initial rendering of layouts can also be time consuming.

For this reason it is important to be considering efficiency when designing layouts. The basic advice given is to only use additional layouts when needed. For example, if the above sample with the three rows put the "First row" and "Second row" *TextViews* in their own *LinearLayout* like how the second row is done, render time would be significantly increased becaused of the additional measurements that have to be made.

5 User Interaction

5.1 Introduction

Now that we have covered layouts in detail, it is only logical that an application should be able to respond to user interaction like button presses, swipes, key presses, and other gestures. All user interaction is processed in the Java code of an Activity with *Listeners*. There are *Listeners* for any kind of interaction, such as *onClickListener* for when a view (such as a button) is pressed, *onTouch* for whenever the user touches the screen, and *onKeyDown* for when a key is pressed, among many different listeners.

The general process for setting up an element of the user interface is to first call *setContentView*, which we have already done to show layouts. Then it is elementary to find views in the layout file set by their IDs. From there, get and set that view's characteristics and assign *Listeners* if needed.

Programmatically changing a view's characteristics can make layouts feel more dynamic than otherwise. For example, on a button press, a *TextView* could change what it says.

5.2   Finding Views

To get a view from the layout shown, use the method *findViewById*, which takes the ID of the view requested and returns a generic *View* object. This may seem bewildering at first, but an example should clear up any confusion.

The layout code used for this example is from the previous chapter when *Rela-*

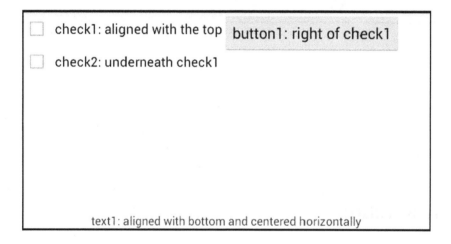

tiveLayout was discussed and produces this layout:

Here is the *onCreate* method from the main activity:

```
@Override
public void onCreate(Bundle savedInstanceState) {
    super.onCreate(savedInstanceState);
    //Set the content view BEFORE finding views
    setContentView(R.layout.activity_main);

    Button button1 = (Button) findViewById(R.id.button1);
}
```

Notice that there is an object *button1* of the class *Button*. Every view that can be defined in XML has a corresponding Java class, so there are also Java classes for *Lin-*

earLayout, RelativeLayout, Checkbox, EditText, TextView, and all the rest. All of these Java classes are subclasses of *View,* so the generic *View* returned by *findViewbyId* can be type casted to a button.

From here, you can access thecharacteristics of the button. Add the following line:

```
button1.setText("Setting Text in Java!");
```

Now, if the app is run, the button's text will no longer be "button1: right of check1", but rather "Setting Text in Java."

Other methods of subclasses of *View* include the ability to set text size and style, dimensions, weight, and alignment, as well as any of the characteristics that can be accessed in an XML layout file.

5.3   Creating Views

In some occasions, it may be necessary (or simpler) to create views in Java, instead of defining them in XML. Any time the layout is complex, like the *RelativeLayout* example, it is highly recommended that the layout be defined in XML.

To create *Views,* it is necessary to have knowledge of *Context.*

5.3.1 Context

Context is an interface that all *Activities* implement. Simply put, *Context* is the means to access resources, the file system, and make system calls (like starting an *Activity*). When working with *AlertDialogs* and anonymously defined classes (*Listeners*), there needs to be a way to access the *Activity*'s *Context.*

The easiest way to accomplish this is to define a *Context* object and in *onCreate,* assign that object to this *Activity.*

```
public class MainActivity extends Activity {

    Context mContext;

    @Override
    public void onCreate(Bundle savedInstanceState) {
        super.onCreate(savedInstanceState);
        setContentView(R.layout.activity_main);
```

```
      mContext = this;
   }

}
```

Now that *Context* has been explained, it is straightforward to create a *View* in Java. This example below shows how to create a *TextView*:

```
TextView text2 = new TextView(mContext);
```

Just like any other object, all that is necessary is to call the constructor. The constructor for any *View* will take the *Context* as an argument. Characteristics of *text2* can be set exactly as they could be in XML.

```
text2.setText("This is some text");
text2.setTextColor(Color.BLUE);
text2.setTypeface(Typeface.create(null, Typeface.BOLD));
```

From here, this *View* can be used for a variety of purposes, such as in a *Dialog* (shown later in this chapter), or even with *setContentView*.

First row

Row 2 Linear Layout   **Button 1**   **Button 2**

Third row

```
setContentView(text2);
```

Just as in XML, it is possible to create more complex layouts. However, there are cases where it will be necessary to declare layouts in Java.

The code example below shows how to create this layout (the XML for this layout is in Chapter 4.7).

```
public void onCreate(Bundle savedInstanceState) {
     super.onCreate(savedInstanceState);

     mContext = this;

     LinearLayout linearVertical = new LinearLayout(mContext);
     linearVertical.setOrientation(LinearLayout.VERTICAL);

     //First Row
     TextView text1 = new TextView(mContext);
     text1.setText("First Row");

     //Second Row
     LinearLayout linearHorizontal = new LinearLayout(mContext);
     linearHorizontal.setOrientation(LinearLayout.HORIZONTAL);

     TextView text2 = new TextView(mContext);
     text2.setText("Row 2 Linear Layout");

     Button button1 = new Button(mContext);
     button1.setText("Button 1");

     Button button2 = new Button(mContext);
     button2.setText("Button 2");

     //Create the second row linear layout
     linearHorizontal.addView(text2);
     linearHorizontal.addView(button1);
     linearHorizontal.addView(button2);

     //Third Row
     TextView text3 = new TextView(mContext);
     text3.setText("Third Row");

     //Adding everything to vertical linear layout
     linearVertical.addView(text1);
     linearVertical.addView(linearHorizontal);
     linearVertical.addView(text3);

     setContentView(linearVertical);
   }
```

At this point, it becomes obvious how inefficient it is to declare layouts in Java as opposed to XML. Anything beyond the simplest of layouts quickly expands to dozens of lines of code and can become difficult to understand. In this example, there is an all-encompassing *LinearLayout* that has three children. The first and third are simply *TextViews*, but the second is another *LinearLayout* with a *TextView* and two *Buttons*.

For the purpose of comparison, the XML that creates the same layout is below.

```xml
<?xml version="1.0" encoding="utf-8"?>
<LinearLayout xmlns:android="http://schemas.android.com/apk/res/android"
    xmlns:tools="http://schemas.android.com/tools"
    android:layout_width="match_parent"
    android:layout_height="match_parent"
    android:orientation="vertical" >

    <TextView
        android:layout_width="wrap_content"
        android:layout_height="wrap_content"
        android:text="First row" />

    <LinearLayout
        android:layout_width="match_parent"
        android:layout_height="wrap_content"
        android:orientation="horizontal" >

        <TextView
            android:layout_width="wrap_content"
            android:layout_height="wrap_content"
            android:text="Row 2 Linear Layout" />

        <Button
            android:layout_width="wrap_content"
            android:layout_height="wrap_content"
            android:text="Button 1" />

        <Button
            android:layout_width="wrap_content"
            android:layout_height="wrap_content"
            android:text="Button 2" />
    </LinearLayout>

    <TextView
        android:layout_width="wrap_content"
        android:layout_height="wrap_content"
        android:text="Third row" />

</LinearLayout>
```

The XML code is slightly shorter and naturally more readable because of the way that children are encapsulated in their parents (as opposed to in Java, where the *addView* method was used to add children to the *LinearLayouts*).

5.4 Listeners

All views have a common set of methods that allow for basic functionality such as setting width and height, padding, whether or not it is visible, disabled (greyed out), how transparent or opaque it is, assigning margins, etc.

Classes of specific views (like *Button*) may have additional methods appropriate to them, such as *ListView*'s *setOnItemSelected* method. For methods like *setOnClick-Listener*, it makes sense that the argument is an object of the class *onClickListener*. All listeners are abstract, so it is necessary to override them. Listeners share the same basic format of containing one method that will be called when an action occurs.

For example, perhaps a *Button* has an *OnClickListener* that will change the button's text. The *OnClickListener* class has one method: *onClick*. So in *onClick*, all that is necessary is one line of code to change the *Button*'s text.

```java
public class MainActivity extends Activity {
    private class MyOnClickListener implements OnClickListener{
        public void onClick(View v) {
            Button b = (Button) v;
            b.setText("This button was pressed!");
        }
    }

    @Override
    public void onCreate(Bundle savedInstanceState) {
        super.onCreate(savedInstanceState);
        //Set the content view BEFORE finding views
        setContentView(R.layout.activity_main);

        Button button1 = (Button) findViewById(R.id.button1);

        button1.setText("Setting Text in Java!");
        button1.setOnClickListener(new MyOnClickListener());
    }

}
```

As can be seen, *MyOnClickListener* is implementing *OnClickListener* and its method *onClick*. Note that *onClick* has an argument of type *View*. This is the view that was clicked. After type casting *v* to a button, the text can be changed. Note that *button1* has its *OnClickListener* set in *onCreate*. *onCreate* is generally where all of the user interface is setup.

Try the above code. The results are as follows.

Before being clicked   **After being clicked**

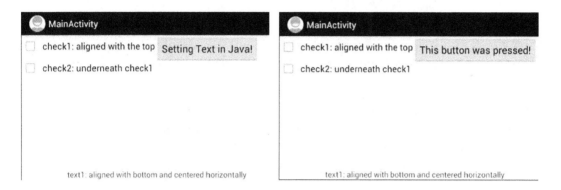

While this code works as expected, the current method of implementing *OnClick-Listener* is clumsy. It is not uncommon to have many views with multiple listeners, so this current method of creating private inner classes will quickly become unmanageable.

A better solution is to use in-line, anonymous class declarations as follows:

```
button1.setOnClickListener(new OnClickListener(){
    public void onClick(View v) {
        Button b = (Button) v;
        b.setText("This button was pressed!");
    }
});
```

This may seem strange and confusing, but it eliminates the need to declare an inner class. In essence, the code defines and constructs an *OnClickListener* with the body contained. Here is the same line of code with the syntax spread out and commented to illustrate how the parenthesis and curly braces are matched.

```
button1.setOnClickListener(
    new OnClickListener() { //create a new OnClickListener
        //implement onClick
        public void onClick(View v) {
            Button b = (Button) v;
            b.setText("This button was pressed!");
        }
    } //end of OnClickListener definition
); //end of the setOnClickListener method
```

At this point, ideally this concept should be clear. If not, there are a myriad of resources available on the internet that may offer further explanation.

Another way to set a *Button*'s functionality is in the XML layout by setting the *onClick* to a method name in the activity. While this may seem more convenient, it can lead to problems very easily, so it is not recommended and should not be used. Also, learning the proper way to set an *OnClickListener* with anonymous classes will make learning other *Listeners* very simple.

5.5   ActionBar and Menu

The *ActionBar* and *Menu* provide a means to keep common actions visible to the user. *ActionBar* was introduced with Android 3.0 and replaced the *Menu* that was used in previous versions of Android. This book will mainly focus on *ActionBar* usage, as it offers additional functionality. At the time of this writing, the current Android version is 4.2. *Menu* was used on Android 2.3 and before. Those earlier versions of Android are obsolete and quickly falling out of use.

Fortunately, the means to populate the *ActionBar* and the *Menu* are exactly the same, although if one desires to maintain compatibility with older devices, the additional functionality from the *ActionBar* cannot be used natively. There are compatibility libraries that will emulate *ActionBar* on older devices (a good example is ActionBarSherlock), but they will not be discussed. From here on, the Menu will not be referred to for the sake of wordiness.

The ActionBar:

The *Menu*:

5.5.1 Populating ActionBar

The *ActionBar* is populated in the *onCreateOptionsMenu* method in an *Activity*. There are two ways to populate an *ActionBar*: the first uses an XML file to declare the items along with their icons and IDs, whereas the second is all in Java.

It is generally recommended that the items be declared in XML, like layouts, because declaring menu items in Java can become clumsy.

To populate the *ActionBar*, override the *onCreateOptionsMenu* method of the *Activity*.

```
@Override
   public boolean onCreateOptionsMenu(Menu menu) {
      MenuInflater inflater = getMenuInflater();
       inflater.inflate(R.menu.activity_main, menu);
      return true;
   }
```

The code here is not very complicated. The object *menu* allows the addition and removal of *ActionBar* items. In this case, a *MenuInflater* is used to "inflate" *menu* with all of the items in the XML file *R.menu.activity_main*.

Create an XML file in *res/menu* if it does not exist already.

In XML, the menu items can be declared as follows:

▲ First Project
  ▷ src
  ▷ gen [Generated Java Files]
  ▷ Android 4.1.2
  ▷ Android Dependencies
    assets
  ▷ bin
  ▷ libs
  ▲ res
    ▷ drawable
    ▷ drawable-hdpi
    ▷ drawable-ldpi
    ▷ drawable-mdpi
    ▷ drawable-xhdpi
    ▷ layout
    ▲ menu
        activity_main.xml
    ▷ values

```
<menu xmlns:android="http://schemas.android.com/apk/res/android" >

    <item
        android:id="@+id/menu_attach"
        android:icon="@drawable/ic_action_attach"
        android:orderInCategory="2"
        android:showAsAction="always"
        android:title="Attach"/>
    <item
        android:id="@+id/menu_search"
        android:icon="@drawable/ic_action_search"
        android:orderInCategory="1"
        android:showAsAction="ifRoom"
        android:title="Search"/>
    <item
        android:id="@+id/menu_settings"
        android:orderInCategory="100"
        android:showAsAction="never"
        android:title="@string/menu_settings"/>

</menu>
```

Each menu item is of the type *item*. There are only a few characteristics available, here are the most important.

The first is *id*, which functions exactly the same as it does with layouts.

Next, *icon* allows an *ActionBar* item to have an icon associated with it. *icon* is optional, and takes an image located in *res/drawable*. Note that in this specific example, the project that we have already setup does not come with the *ic_action_search* drawable, which was added manually. To add icons to an application, simply drop an image into the *drawable* folders. This is covered along with icon design in the last chapter.

orderInCategory sets the order each item should be in in the *ActionBar*.

showAsAction determines if a menu item should be in the main *ActionBar* always, only if there is room left in the *ActionBar*, or if it should always be put into the overflow menu.

Finally, *title* sets the text of the menu item.

Here is what this menu looks like.

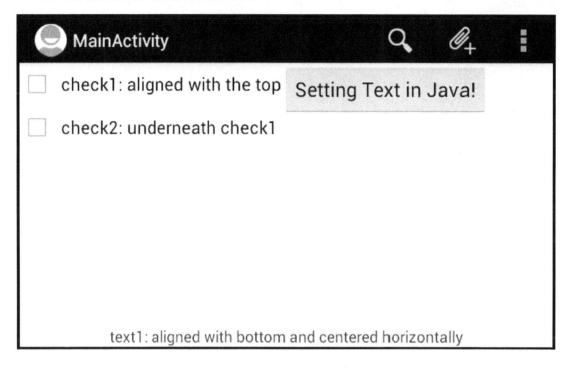

5.6 Responding to ActionBar Item Presses

To accept *ActionBar Item* presses, simply override *onOptionsItemSelected* in an *Activity*. The only argument for this method is a *MenuItem*, which contains information about the *MenuItem* that was clicked, such as the item's ID, title, and icon.

It is common to have multiple items in the *ActionBar*, so the best way to sort through which item was selected is through a switch statement corresponding to the item's ID. See the example below.

```
@Override
   public boolean onOptionsItemSelected(MenuItem item) {
      TextView text = (TextView) findViewById(R.id.text1);

      switch(item.getItemId()){
      case R.id.menu_attach:
        //functionality for the "attach" menu item
        text.setText("Attach a file");
        return true;
      case R.id.menu_search:
        //functionality for the "search" menu item
        text.setText("Perform a Search");
```

```
        return true;
    case R.id.menu_settings:
        //functionality for the "settings" menu item
        text.setText("Go to settings");
        return true;
    }

    return false;
}
```

In this example, the switch statement determines which case to run based on the *MenuItem*'s ID and appropriately selects the case with a matching ID.

In these simple cases, the *TextView* at the bottom of the screen will change its text as the different *MenuItem*s are pressed. Obviously, in a real application, pressing an *Item* in the *ActionBar* will probably do more than simply setting a *TextView*'s text, but this example shows how and where to add functionality.

5.7 Dialogs

Dialogs are an integral part of any interface. Their primary uses are to notify the user of an event, allow for a selection or choice to be made, or to simply display a small amount of information.

Fortunately, Android has a very fully featured *AlertDialog* class that can be used to create and display dialogs. When dealing with dialogs, you will need a reference to *Context*.

First off, the way to create a dialog is as follows:

```
AlertDialog diag = new AlertDialog.Builder(mContext).create();
        diag.setTitle("My title");
        diag.setMessage("My message");
        diag.setIcon(R.drawable.ic_launcher);
        //After Configuring the dialog, show it
        diag.show();
```

The *Builder* class in *AlertDialog* is used to construct the *AlertDialog*, and requires a reference to *Context* to access resources.

After building the *AlertDialog*, you can set its characteristics, such as the title, message, and buttons (if any).

Note that when setting buttons, a standard *OnClickListener* (in the *View* class) is not used. Instead a *DialogInterface.OnClickListener* (in the *DialogInterface* class) must be used to accept *AlertDialog* button presses. This is because AlertDialog itself implements *DialogInterface*, not *View*. It seems to be a minor detail, but using a *View.OnClickListener* will not work. An example on how to set buttons is shown below:

```
diag.setButton(DialogInterface.BUTTON_POSITIVE, "Okay",
        new DialogInterface.OnClickListener() {
    public void onClick(DialogInterface dialog
                    , int which) {
        //Add functionality here
      }
   });
    diag.setButton(DialogInterface.BUTTON_NEGATIVE, "Cancel",
        new DialogInterface.OnClickListener() {
    public void onClick(DialogInterface dialog
                    , int which) {
        //Clicking a button in a dialog automatically
        //closes the dialog, so there is no need to do
        //anything if the "Cancel" button is clicked
      }
   });
```

setButton adds a button to the dialog. The arguments for *setButton* are an *int* that can be found in *DialogInterface* that corresponds to whether the button is positive, negative, or neutral, the text for the button, and finally the *OnClickListener*. The positive, negative, or neutral values will determine how the buttons are laid out; furthermore, there cannot be more than one positive button on a dialog (likewise with negative and neutral buttons).

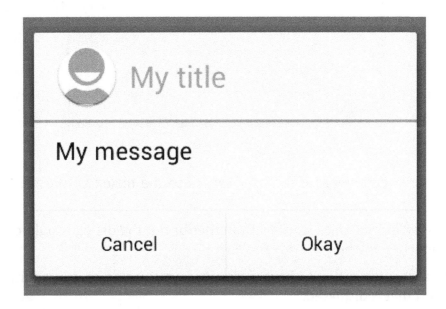

Some additional methods that may be useful are shown as follows:

```
diag.setCanceledOnTouchOutside(true);
diag.setCancelable(true);
EditText inputText = new EditText(mContext);
diag.setView(inputText);
```

setCancelable determines if the user can close the dialog by pressing the back button.

setCanceledOnTouchOutside will set whether or not the dialog should close when the users touches anything outside the dialog.

setView allows the dialog to have a view or layout inside of it in addition to the message text that is displayed.

Finally, for cases where the dialog has to be manually closed in code, the *hide* method can be used.

```
diag.hide();
```

5.7.1 Use Cases For Dialogs

A *Dialog* is typically used to notify users of something important, prompt for a choice or input, ask for a confirmation, or give the user an option to take or cancel an action.

Here is an actual use for a dialog with an *EditText* inside.

In this case, clicking the "Attach" menu option will open a dialog, which prompts the user to input a message. When the positive button labeled "Okay" is pressed, text1 (the TextView at the bottom of the layout) has its text set to the text from the EditText in the Dialog which is retrieved by using the getText method.

The flow of the user interface is shown on the next page. The code for this example follows.

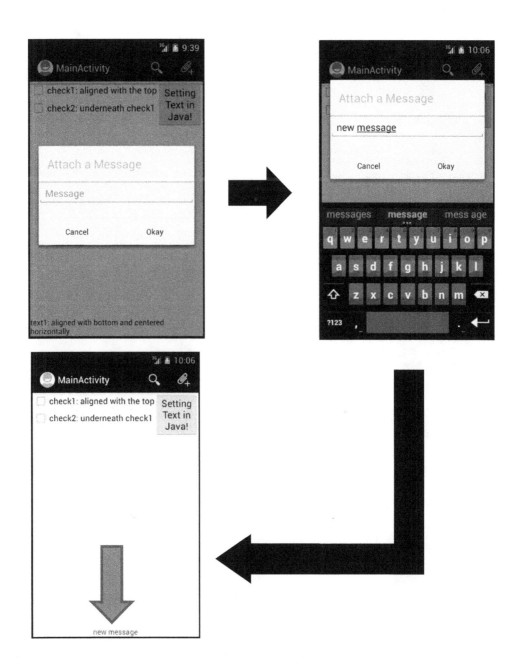

```java
public class MainActivity extends Activity {

   Context mContext;
   TextView text1;

   @Override
   public void onCreate(Bundle savedInstanceState) {
      super.onCreate(savedInstanceState);
      // Set the content view BEFORE finding views
      setContentView(R.layout.activity_main);

      mContext = this;

      text1 = (TextView)findViewById(R.id.text1);

   }

   @Override
   public boolean onCreateOptionsMenu(Menu menu) {
      MenuInflater inflater = getMenuInflater();
        inflater.inflate(R.menu.activity_main, menu);
        return true;
   }

   @Override
   public boolean onOptionsItemSelected(MenuItem item) {
       TextView text = (TextView) findViewById(R.id.text1);

       switch(item.getItemId()){
       case R.id.menu_attach:
          AlertDialog diag = new AlertDialog.Builder(mContext).create();
          diag.setTitle("Attach a Message");
          final EditText inputText = new EditText(mContext);
          inputText.setHint("Message");
          diag.setView(inputText);

          diag.setButton(DialogInterface.BUTTON_POSITIVE, "Okay",
                new DialogInterface.OnClickListener() {
             public void onClick(DialogInterface dialog, int which) {
                String input = inputText.getText().toString();
                text1.setText(input);
             }
          });
          diag.setButton(DialogInterface.BUTTON_NEGATIVE, "Cancel",
                new DialogInterface.OnClickListener() {
             public void onClick(DialogInterface dialog, int which) {
                //Clicking a button in a dialog
                //automatically closes
                //the dialog, so there is no need to do
                //anything if the "Cancel" button is clicked
             }
          });
```

```
        //After Configuring the dialog, show it
        diag.show();

        return true;
    case R.id.menu_search:
        //"search" menu item
        text.setText("Perform a Search");
        return true;
    case R.id.menu_settings:
        //"settings" menu item
        text.setText("Go to settings");
        return true;
    }

    return false;
    }

}
```

Note that all of the code related to creating, setting up, and showing the dialog occurs when the *menu_attach* item is pressed.

Also, pay special attention to getting text from an *EditText*. *getText* does not return a *String*, it returns and *Editable*, which is similar to a *String*, but is mutable and can be changed after it is created.

Nevertheless, *setText* on *text1* takes a *String* as an argument, so it is necessary to call *toString* on the *Editable*.

This simple example demonstrates accepting user input in *Dialog*s. The same general procedure of getting input and changing parts of the interface will be used extensively throughout user interface design.

6 Advanced Interface Design

6.1 Introduction

Given the tools and methods shown so far to build an app, there is only so much a developer could do. There are fairly common parts of an interface that we have not covered yet that will be explained.

This chapter covers creating navigation methods (such as tabs and dropdown lists), having multiple activities, using the intent system, and using more advanced views (like *ListView*) will be covered, along with other miscellaneous topics, such as *Preferences* and *AnimationBuilder*.

After completing this chapter, all the tools needed to create a typical user experience on Android have been demonstrated.

6.2   Navigation

The two most important parts of an application are its feature set and its navigation within the app. Simply stated, if an application is difficult to use, then most users will not find it useful. An interface has to be straightforward and clean. It is best to avoid adding additional clutter without hiding features.

The most essential feature of this design is the workflow within an application. The process a user must take to perform an action should make sense and seem intuitive even to someone who has never seen the app before.

Most applications are broken down into distinct screens that can be navigated through by one of several methods: tabs, a dropdown list, or swipeable pages.

6.2.1 Tabs

Tabs are very common and familiar to users of almost every computing platform (whether it is mobile or desktop operating system). Tabs are useful for separating distinct features of an application. For example, an eBook store application might have two tabs: one that shows the user's library of books, and another to browse and buy books.

Unfortunately, after three or four tabs, the app becomes unwieldy. Android

is smart enough to make the tab list scrollable once tabs extend past the screen, but a large number of tabs will not be an ideal solution due to the more cluttered and unclear interface.

6.2.2 **Swipeable Pages**

Swipeable pages are an Android specific interface convention. Swipeable pages appear in two forms: in combination with tabs, or with a title strip. When using swipeable pages with tabs, the graphical interface looks the same as if normal tabs were used (with the exception that the tabs can be swiped between). The title strip implementation is shown below.

Before Swiping   Mid-Swipe   After Swiping

Swipeable tabs are cleaner than tabs because having four or five swipeable pages is more manageable for the user than four or five tabs. The downside to swipeable pages is that a user has to swipe through all of the pages to get to the very last one, which is a problem that tabs and lists avoid.

For developers, creating swipeable tabs involves slightly more overhead code than normal tabs and lists, but the added functionality is worth the additional code.

6.2.3 **Lists**

Lists, unlike tabs and swipeable pages, are a good choice for displaying many options. Of course, beyond some point, even a list will become overwhelming to a user, but it is not uncommon for a list to have up to ten choices.

List Collapsed   List Expanded

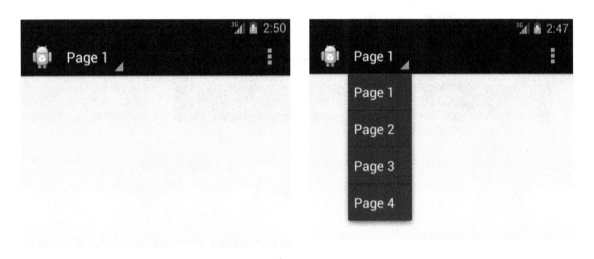

6.3   **Fragments**

As layouts become more complicated and develop more fully featured navigation, *Fragments* will allow the user interface to be broken into reusable pieces. To a beginning Android developer, this may seem unnecessary, but *Fragments* can showcase how easily an app built for phones can be made to work well on tablets as well. Furthermore, *Fragments* are required to use tabs and the swipeable pages.

Fragments are more than just layouts. If anything, a *Fragment* is similar to an *Activity*. A *Fragment* has an *onCreateView* (as opposed to *onCreate*), *onPause*, *onResume*, *onSaveInstanceState*, and many other methods similar or identical to an *Activity*.

However, just because a *Fragment* has the same methods as an *Activity* does not make it an *Activity*. A *Fragment* is useless without an overall *Activity* handling it. For example, an *Activity* will have to instantiate a *Fragment* and pass data into the *Fragment*, as well as perform a transaction to place the *Fragment* on the screen.

As mentioned earlier, common use cases of *Fragments* include easy optimization of an app for both phones and tablets, as well as more convenient use of swipeable pages and tabs. Most applications are broken into two pages. One includes a list of items. Upon clicking on one of the items, the user is brought to another page with details of that item. On a tablet, it would make sense that the list is one pane on the left of the screen, and the details would be a pane on the right of the screen. However, on a phone, the list and details should be displayed on their own individual screens.

The solution in this case is to make both the list page and the details page into *Fragments*. At runtime it is possible to determine screen size. If the screen is bigger than 6.5 inches (threshold for a tablet), then clicking one of the items in the list *Fragment*, should add a corresponding details *Fragment* to the right of the screen. Otherwise, if the screen is not large enough to be considered a tablet, have the details *Fragment* occupy the whole screen. Optimizing for both tablets and phones will be covered in the next chapter.

Here is some simple *Fragment* code:

```
public class MyFragment extends Fragment{

    @Override
    public View onCreateView(LayoutInflater inflater, ViewGroup container,
        Bundle savedInstanceState) {
      //Inflate the layout, leave the container argument null
      View layout = inflater.inflate(R.layout.activity_main, null);
```

```
      //setup buttons and other views here
      TextView text =
              (TextView) layout.findViewById(R.id.fragment_textview);
      text.setText("Hello!");

      //Return the layout at the end
      return layout;
   }
}
```

Writing a *Fragment* is very similar to an *Activity*, but there are some key differences. First, note that the example *MyFragment* extends *Fragment* instead of *Activity*. Also, pay attention to *onCreateView*. Whereas in *onCreate* in an *Activity* the method *setContentView* is called to set the layout, *Fragments* return a *View* in *onCreateView*.

There is one minor difference between *setContentView* and returning a *View*: *setContentView* can take either a *View* object or a resource (such as *R.layout.activity_main*). *onCreateView* can only return a *View* object, so in order to use a resource, it will have to be inflated into a *View* object.

Thankfully, one of the arguments of *onCreateView* is a *LayoutInflater*, which can easily create a *View* from a resource.

One further small difference is when calling *findViewById* to get views in the layout, the method must be called on the inflated *View* object. The reason why this is not necessary in an *Activity* is that *findViewById* is called on the *View* passed in through *setContentView*.

6.4 Using Fragments

At this point, it is time to start using *Fragments*. Create a new Android Application Project named *"Fragment Example"*. Make sure that the minimum SDK version is API 11 or above. Next, create a new XML layout with a *TextView* in it. Create a new Java source file named *TextFragment*; make sure that it extends

Fragment. Copy the above *onCreateView* code into *TextFragment*'s *onCreateView*. Change the layout resource name and the *TextView* id if necessary.

In *activity_main.xml*, add a *FrameLayout* that occupies the entire screen. By itself, a *FrameLayout* does nothing (similar to *LinearLayout,* or *RelativeLayout,* which only serve to position their children). This *FrameLayout* will serve to contain a *TextFragment* at runtime.

Adding or swapping a *Fragment* into a layout at runtime is straightforward thanks to the *FragmentManager* class. Here is the *onCreate* for *MainActivity* that will add a new *TextFragment* to the *FrameLayout* that was added earlier in *activity_main.xml*.

```
@Override
protected void onCreate(Bundle savedInstanceState) {
    super.onCreate(savedInstanceState);
    setContentView(R.layout.activity_main);

    getFragmentManager()
        .beginTransaction()
        .replace(R.id.fragment_frame, new TextFragment())
        .commit();
}
```

getFragmentManager will return a *FragmentManager*. The process of swapping a *Fragment* into a layout involves first beginning a transaction, then calling *add* or *replace* to put a *Fragment* as a child of a *View*, and finally committing the change. The difference between *add* and *replace* is that *add* will put another *Fragment* in the specified container *View*, whereas *replace* will wipe all the *Fragments* in the container and then add another *Fragment*. *add* can lead to *Fragments* overlapping each other, so in almost all cases *replace* should be used.

At this point, try running the application. "Hello!" should appear on the screen. This is an oversimplified use of a *Fragment*, but it demonstrates how to implement *Fragments*. In most scenarios, a *Fragment* is passed a number of arguments and is used to quickly lay out information. Passing and receiving arguments is relatively simple, but makes use of the *Bundle* class. *Bundle* is very similar to *Map*, so it should not be difficult to learn.

One key difference between a *Bundle* and a *Map* is that a *Bundle* can only accept certain data types. A *Bundle* can contain all of the primitive types, arrays of primitives, *Strings*, *ArrayList<String>*, and subclasses of the *Parcelable* interface (which will not be covered here).

To put items into a *Bundle*, use methods like *putString* or *putDoubleArray*. The "put" methods take two arguments. The first is a String that acts like a key (which functions exactly the same as it does in a *Map*), and the second argument is that object or primitive to be passed in.

Getting items from a *Bundle* is a similar process. The "get" methods (like *getString*, or *getInt*) only take one argument: the key for the item to be retrieved. If the item requested does not exist in the *Bundle*, null will be returned (or a default value if the item is a primitive).

Another important method of *Bundle* is *containsKey*.

To make the *TextFragment* class more useful, it will have to accept arguments that can be passed in.

```
public class TextFragment extends Fragment{

    @Override
    public View onCreateView(LayoutInflater inflater, ViewGroup container,
        Bundle savedInstanceState) {
        //Inflate the layout
        View layout = inflater.inflate(R.layout.my_layout, null);

        //setup buttons and other views here
        TextView text = (TextView) layout.findViewById
                                        (R.id.fragment_textview);


        Bundle arguments = getArguments();

        //if arguments is null,
        //then there are no arguments,
        //check to see if there are any
```

```
      //arguments to avoid a NullPointerException
      //when calling arguments.containsKey
      if(arguments != null){
         if(arguments.containsKey("text")){
            //The bundle contains an argument
            //called "text", so set the TextView
            text.setText(arguments.getString("text"));
         }else{
            //There is no "text" argument
            text.setText("No text availible");
         }
      }else{
         //There were no arguments
         text.setText("No text availible");
      }

      return layout;
   }

}
```

At this point the *TextFragment* is beginning to become useful. It is typical for a *Fragment* to be passed multiple arguments. Passing in arguments is relatively straightforward and involves creating a *Bundle* and putting values into it.

The following code is the *onCreate* method in *MainActivity*.

```
   @Override
   protected void onCreate(Bundle savedInstanceState) {
      super.onCreate(savedInstanceState);
      setContentView(R.layout.activity_main);

      //create a new TextFragment
      TextFragment textFrag1 = new TextFragment();

//Arguments are passed in in a Bundle
//so create a Bundle and put in arguments
      Bundle arguments = new Bundle();
      arguments.putString("text", "This text was passed as an argument");

      //Set the TextFragment's arguments before performing
      //a transaction
      textFrag1.setArguments(arguments);
```

```
        getFragmentManager()
          .beginTransaction()
          .add(R.id.fragment_frame, textFrag1)
          .commit();
      }
```

Try running the application. The "This text was passed in as an argument" text should appear on the screen. Now that Fragments have been explained, navigation methods like tabs and swipeable pages can be implemented.

6.5   Implementing Navigation

The three primary forms of Navigation are all implemented with the help of *ActionBar*, which has built in support for tabs and lists. As for the swipeable pages, a view called a *ViewPager* will be used.

6.5.1 Implementing Tabs

Tabs are the simplest of the three to use (from the standpoint of a developer), so they will be explained first. Tabs are especially suited for *Fragments*,

The best way to understand how to use tabs is by seeing a code example.

```java
public class MainActivity extends Activity {

  @Override
  protected void onCreate(Bundle savedInstanceState) {
    super.onCreate(savedInstanceState);
    setContentView(R.layout.activity_main);

    //Get the ActionBar
    ActionBar actionBar = getActionBar();

    //Set the ActionBar to use tabs
    actionBar.setNavigationMode(ActionBar.NAVIGATION_MODE_TABS);

    //create a TabListeneer that will handle
```

```
//tab selections

ActionBar.TabListener tabListener = new ActionBar.TabListener() {
    @Override
    public void onTabUnselected(Tab tab, FragmentTransaction ft) {
        // This small example has nothing to do when
        //a tab is unselected
    }
    @Override
    public void onTabSelected(Tab tab, FragmentTransaction ft) {
        switch(tab.getPosition()){
            case 0:
                    //This is the first tab
                    TextFragment textFrag1 = new TextFragment();

                    Bundle arguments1 = new Bundle();
                    arguments1.putString("text",
                                                "This is the first tab");
                    textFrag1.setArguments(arguments1);

                    ft.replace(R.id.fragment_frame, textFrag1);
                    break;

            case 1:
                    //This is the second tab
                    TextFragment textFrag2 = new TextFragment();

                    Bundle arguments2 = new Bundle();
                    arguments2.putString("text",
                                            "This is the second tab");
                    textFrag2.setArguments(arguments2);

                    ft.replace(R.id.fragment_frame, textFrag2);
                    break;
        }
    }
    @Override
    public void onTabReselected(Tab tab, FragmentTransaction ft) {
        //This example has nothing to do when
        //a tab is reselected
    }
};

//Create the two tabs
ActionBar.Tab tab1 = actionBar.newTab();
tab1.setText("Tab 1");
```

```java
    tab1.setTabListener(tabListener);

    ActionBar.Tab tab2 = actionBar.newTab();
    tab2.setText("Tab 2");
    tab2.setTabListener(tabListener);

    //add the tabs to the actionbar
    actionBar.addTab(tab1);
    actionBar.addTab(tab2);
  }

  @Override
  public boolean onCreateOptionsMenu(Menu menu) {
    // Inflate the menu; this adds items to the action bar if it is
present.
    getMenuInflater().inflate(R.menu.activity_main, menu);
    return true;
  }

}
```

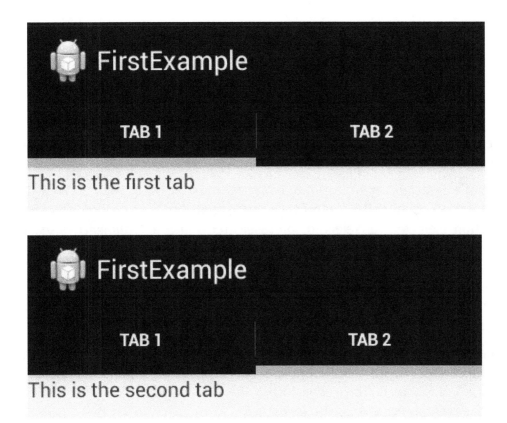

This example code shows how to use tabs. There may seem to be a lot of code in this example, but it is straightforward and not very complicated, as most of the setup consists of writing listeners.[3] Here is a detailed explanation of the code.

First *super.onCreate* and *setContentView* are called, as always. Next a reference to the *ActionBar* must be obtained. After getting the *ActionBar*, the *Ac-*

---

[3] This kind of code is often referred to by developers as "boilerplate" because it will be used repetitively for the same purpose.

tionBar is told that tabs will be used in the method *setNavigationMode*. *Action-Bar.NAVIGATION_MODE_TABS* is a static, constant integer.

Next, an *ActionBar.TabListener* must be created. A *TabListener* receives calls when tabs are selected, unselected, or reselected. In some applications, it may be necessary to add functionality when tabs are unselected or reselected. For example, suppose a text editor application can open multiple files in separate tabs. When a tab (text file) is unselected, the application should save changes made. In the tab demonstration example, there is nothing to do when a tab is unselected or reselected.

In *onTabSelected*, an appropriate *Fragment* must be swapped into view. The arguments for each method in a *TabListener* are always the tab that is receiving the action (selected, unselected, or reselected), and a *FragmentTransaction*, which makes swapping *Fragments* easy. When determining which *Fragment* to display, it is common to use the position of the tab. The *getPosition* method of a *Tab* returns the tab's index. Index is determined by the order in which the tabs are added. The first tab added (left-most tab when displayed) is always at position 0. From there, the next tab to the right is one position higher.

The *switch* statement determines which *Fragment* to display and then swapping the correct *Fragment* in is simply a matter of setting arguments and using the supplied *FragmentTransaction* to put the new *Fragment* into the frame by using the *replace* method, as shown earlier.

6.5.2 Implementing List Navigation

Lists are implemented in a similar manner to tabs, with one significant difference: instead of adding choices (tabs or lists) individually, an *Adapter* is used. *Adapters* are used to create *Views* from some form of data. For example, the *ArrayAdapter* class can be used to create *TextViews* from an *ArrayList<String>* or *String[]*.

In the case with list navigation, it is common to use an *ArrayAdapter*. Below is the source for simple list navigation.

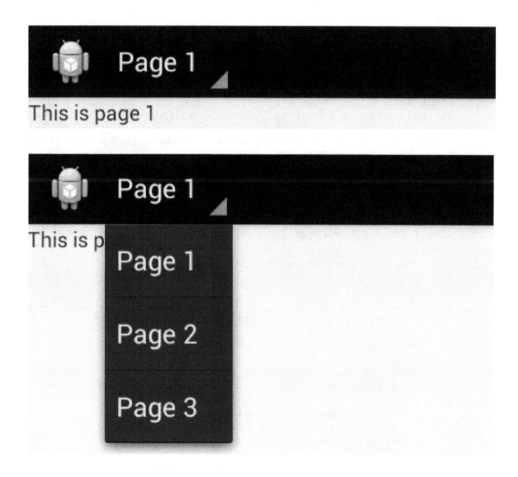

```
public class MainActivity extends FragmentActivity {

    @Override
    protected void onCreate(Bundle savedInstanceState) {
        super.onCreate(savedInstanceState);
        setContentView(R.layout.activity_main);
```

```java
//Get the ActionBar
ActionBar actionBar = getActionBar();

//Not showing the application name generally
//looks better when using list navigation
actionBar.setDisplayShowTitleEnabled(false);

//Use list navigation
actionBar.setNavigationMode(ActionBar.NAVIGATION_MODE_LIST);

//The list of selectable items
String[] pages = { "Page 1", "Page 2", "Page 3" };

ArrayAdapter<String> listItemAdapter = new ArrayAdapter<String>(
    actionBar.getThemedContext(),
            //use the ActionBar's context
    android.R.layout.simple_list_item_1,
    pages);

//Create the listener for when items
//in the list are selected
ActionBar.OnNavigationListener listListener =
    new ActionBar.OnNavigationListener() {

  @Override
  public boolean onNavigationItemSelected(int position, long id) {
      //Determine which Fragment to display based on
      //position of the item
      switch(position){
      case 0:
          //This is the first page
          TextFragment textFrag1 = new TextFragment();

          Bundle arguments1 = new Bundle();
          arguments1.putString("text", "This is page 1");
          textFrag1.setArguments(arguments1);

          getFragmentManager().beginTransaction()
                            .replace(R.id.fragment_frame,
                                                    textFrag1)
                            .commit();
      break;

      case 1:
          //This is the second page
          TextFragment textFrag2 = new TextFragment();
```

```
                Bundle arguments2 = new Bundle();
                arguments2.putString("text", "This is page 2");
                textFrag2.setArguments(arguments2);

                getFragmentManager().beginTransaction()
                            .replace(R.id.fragment_frame, textFrag2)
                            .commit();
                break;

            case 2:
                //This is the third page
                TextFragment textFrag3 = new TextFragment();

                Bundle arguments3 = new Bundle();
                arguments3.putString("text", "This is page 3");
                textFrag3.setArguments(arguments3);

                //Set the fragment
                getFragmentManager().beginTransaction()
                            .replace(R.id.fragment_frame, textFrag3)
                            .commit();
                break;
            }
            return true;
        }
    };

    //Set the item adapter and the listener
    actionBar.setListNavigationCallbacks(listItemAdapter, listListener);
    }

    @Override
    public boolean onCreateOptionsMenu(Menu menu) {
        //Inflate the menu; this adds items to the action bar if it is
        //present.
        getMenuInflater().inflate(R.menu.activity_main, menu);
        return true;
    }
}
```

listItemAdapter is the *Adapter* that will translate the *String* array *pages* into *TextViews*. The arguments taken by the *ArrayAdapter* constructor are a *Context*, an XML layout, and finally the *ArrayList* or *Array* that contains the data to be entered into the XML layout.

In the example code, for *Context, actionBar.getThemedContext( )* is used. It is wise to use the *ActionBar*'s *Context* instead of the *Activity*'s *Context* because the *ActionBar* may be themed differently than the rest of the application. For example, it is common for the bulk of an application to have a light background with dark text, but to have the *ActionBar* have a dark background with light text. In this described situation, using the *Activity*'s *Context* would result in the *ActionBar* list navigation having dark text on a dark background (which would be unreadable).

The XML layout resource used is *android.R.layout.simple_list_item_1*, which is simply a *TextView*. Note that this resource does not belong to the application, but rather is built into Android (it uses *android.R* instead of *R*, which is generated for each individual application's resources). The source for *layout_simple_list_item_1* is below:

```
<!--
 Copyright (C) 2006 The Android Open Source Project

     Licensed under the Apache License, Version 2.0 (the "License");
     you may not use this file except in compliance with the License.
     You may obtain a copy of the License at

          http://www.apache.org/licenses/LICENSE-2.0

     Unless required by applicable law or agreed to in writing, software
     distributed under the License is distributed on an "AS IS" BASIS,
     WITHOUT WARRANTIES OR CONDITIONS OF ANY KIND, either express or im-
plied.
     See the License for the specific language governing permissions and
     limitations under the License.
-->
<TextView xmlns:android="http://schemas.android.com/apk/res/android"
    android:id="@android:id/text1"
    android:layout_width="fill_parent"
    android:layout_height="wrap_content"
    android:gravity="center_vertical"
    android:minHeight="?android:attr/listPreferredItemHeight"
```

```
android:paddingLeft="6dip"
android:textAppearance="?android:attr/textAppearanceLarge" />
```

An *ArrayAdapter* object simply tries to set the text of *text1* in the layout given to it to a member of the *Array* or *ArrayList* passed to it. Therefore, if a developer wanted to, it is possible to declare one's own list item XML layout with different styling from *layout_simple_list_item_1*. Furthermore, it is possible to create a custom *Adapter*. For example, perhaps in a messaging application's contact list a list item should have an *ImageView* (for the contact's picture) and a *TextView* (for the contact's name). Custom adapters are a slightly more advanced topic, and custom *Adapters* will be shown when lists are covered in more detail.

As for setting the *Fragment* to be displayed, instead of using a *TabListener*, an *OnNavigationListener* is selected. Unlike *TabListener*, *OnNavigationListener* does not have methods for when a page is unselected or reselected, and does not have a *FragmentTransaction* as an argument. In *onNavigationItemSelected*, the *Fragment* to be displayed is determined by using the position of the list item selected. This is the same trick that was used when implementing tabs. After entering a case in the *switch* statement, the code looks largely the same as it did with the tab interface. The only exception is that because a *FragmentTransaction* was not passed in, *getFragmentManager( ).beginTransaction( )* must be called.

Now that the *Adapter* and the *Listener* have been setup, it is time to call *setListNavigationCallbacks*, which takes the *Adapter* and *Listener* as arguments. This concludes setup of *ActionBar* list navigation.

6.5.3 Implementing Swipeable Pages

Swipeable pages are implemented significantly differently from tab and list navigation. The first step is to add the Android support library. The support library was created to add additional functionality to both previous versions of Android, as well as future revisions. Adding the support library is easy, simply right click on the Eclipse project, go to "Android Tools," and click "Add Support Library..." If the support library has not already been downloaded, a prompt will appear asking to accept the license agreements and install the library.

Now that that has been done, replace the *FrameLayout* in the *activity_main.xml* file with *android.support.v4.view.ViewPager*. Also, it is a good idea to change the id to something more appropriate than "fragment_container" which was used in the last example (this example will use "viewpager"). *ViewPager* is a more advanced *View* that takes an *Adapter* in a similar way to how list navigation worked.

Instead of an *ArrayAdapter*, a *FragmentPagerAdapter* will be used. Because the support library will be used, there are a few changes to be made before adding swipe navigation. First, open the *TextFragment* class. In the imports, change the import *android.app.Fragment* to *android.support.v4.app.Fragment*. The support library has its own version of *Fragments* and it is necessary to use the support library's version. Also, in the *MainActivity* java file, change *extends Activity* to *extends FragmentActivity*. This changes some methods to work nicely with the support *Fragments*. For example, the method *getFragmentManager* will now be written as *getSupportFragmentManager*. Just as with the *TextFragment* class, remove imports such as *android.app.Fragment* and *android.app.FragmentManager*. Instead, use the support library versions of these classes.

Here is the code to show three different *TextFragments* that can be swiped through:

```
public class MainActivity extends FragmentActivity {

    @Override
    protected void onCreate(Bundle savedInstanceState) {
        super.onCreate(savedInstanceState);
        setContentView(R.layout.activity_main);

        FragmentManager fragManager = getSupportFragmentManager();
        FragmentPagerAdapter fragAdapter =
```

```java
                              new FragmentPagerAdapter(fragManager){

    @Override
    public int getCount() {
       //The number of pages that
       //there will be
       return 3;
    }

    @Override
    public Fragment getItem(int position) {
       switch(position){
       case 0:
          //This is the first page
          TextFragment textFrag1 = new TextFragment();

          Bundle arguments1 = new Bundle();
          arguments1.putString("text", "This is page 1");
          textFrag1.setArguments(arguments1);

          return textFrag1;
       case 1:
          //This is the second page
          TextFragment textFrag2 = new TextFragment();

          Bundle arguments2 = new Bundle();
          arguments2.putString("text", "This is page 2");
          textFrag2.setArguments(arguments2);

          return textFrag2;
       case 2:
          //This is the third page
          TextFragment textFrag3 = new TextFragment();

          Bundle arguments3 = new Bundle();
          arguments3.putString("text", "This is page 3");
          textFrag3.setArguments(arguments3);

          return  textFrag3;
       }
       return null;
    }
};

//Find the ViewPager in the layout
ViewPager pager = (ViewPager) findViewById(R.id.viewpager);
```

```
    //Set the ViewPager's adapter
    //to display the TextFragments
    pager.setAdapter(fragAdapter);

}


@Override
public boolean onCreateOptionsMenu(Menu menu) {
    // Inflate the menu; this adds items to the action bar if it is
    // present.
    getMenuInflater().inflate(R.menu.activity_main, menu);
    return true;
}

}
```

Try running the application and swiping through the pages. At this point, there is no indication that the pages can be swiped through. This is most commonly accomplished through the use of a *PagerTitleStrip*. The layout code should look like this:

```
<RelativeLayout
xmlns:android="http://schemas.android.com/apk/res/android"
    xmlns:tools="http://schemas.android.com/tools"
    android:layout_width="match_parent"
    android:layout_height="match_parent"
    tools:context=".MainActivity" >

    <android.support.v4.view.ViewPager
        android:id="@+id/viewpager"
        android:layout_width="match_parent"
        android:layout_height="match_parent" >

        <android.support.v4.view.PagerTitleStrip
            android:id="@+id/pager_title_strip"
            android:layout_width="match_parent"
            android:layout_height="wrap_content"
            android:layout_gravity="top"
            android:background="#33b5e5"
```

```
                android:paddingBottom="4dp"
                android:paddingTop="4dp"
                android:textColor="#fff" />

    </android.support.v4.view.ViewPager>

</RelativeLayout>
```

Be sure that the *PagerTitleStrip* is a child of the *ViewPager*. The colors of the *PagerTitleStrip* can be adjusted by changing the *textcolor* and *background* values.

In the *MainActivity*, in the *FragmentPagerAdapter*, another method is needed to return page titles. Override the *getPageTitle* method and return an appropriate title (as a *String)* for each page. Here is the new *FragmentPagerAdapter*:

```
FragmentPagerAdapter fragAdapter = new FragmentPagerAdapter(fragManager)
{

    @Override
    public int getCount() {
        //The number of pages that
        //there will be
        return 3;
    }

    @Override
    public Fragment getItem(int position) {
        switch(position){
        case 0:
            //This is the first page
            TextFragment textFrag1 = new TextFragment();

            Bundle arguments1 = new Bundle();
            arguments1.putString("text", "This is page 1");
            textFrag1.setArguments(arguments1);

            return textFrag1;
        case 1:
            //This is the second page
```

```java
        TextFragment textFrag2 = new TextFragment();

        Bundle arguments2 = new Bundle();
        arguments2.putString("text", "This is page 2");
        textFrag2.setArguments(arguments2);

        return textFrag2;
    case 2:
        //This is the third page
        TextFragment textFrag3 = new TextFragment();

        Bundle arguments3 = new Bundle();
        arguments3.putString("text", "This is page 3");
        textFrag3.setArguments(arguments3);

        return  textFrag3;
    }
    return null;
}


@Override
public CharSequence getPageTitle(int position){
    switch(position){
    case 0:
        return "Page 1";
    case 1:
        return "Page 2";
    case 2:
        return "Page 3";
    }

    //This code should never be reached,
    //because getCount() should
    //always return that there
    //are 3 pages
    return "";
  }
};
```

Run the application. It should be much more user friendly now that there is an indication that there are multiple pages.

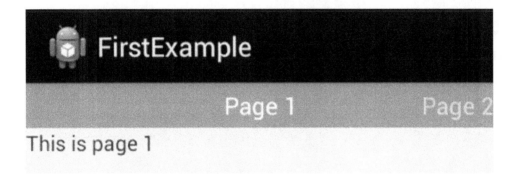

6.6   Views with Adapters

Some *Views* are meant to show data that can be easily changed or loaded during runtime. Specifically, *ListView* and *GridView* are meant to showcase a group of data.

ListView example: *GridView* example:

First Project
Item 0
Item 1
Item 2
Item 3
Item 4
Item 5
Item 6
Item 7
Item 8

First Project	
Item 0	Item 1
Item 2	Item 3
Item 4	Item 5
Item 6	Item 7
Item 8	Item 9

In practice, *ListView* and *GridView* can be used interchangeably. When deciding which to use, consider how much data will be displayed in an item. In the above example, the *ListView* implementation has a lot of whitespace to the right of each item, which is not idea. *GridView* is also better suited at scaling to larger screen sizes, because it can automatically adjust the number of columns based on screen width and the width of items. For example, in portrait orientation, *GridView* might have two columns, but in landscape orientation, three columns might be shown. On a tablet, a *GridView* might expand to four columns if there is room.

6.6.1 Implementing ListView

First, you will needa ListView in the main XML layout file, as shown here:

```
<RelativeLayout
xmlns:android="http://schemas.android.com/apk/res/android"
    xmlns:tools="http://schemas.android.com/tools"
    android:layout_width="match_parent"
    android:layout_height="match_parent"
    tools:context=".MainActivity" >

    <ListView
        android:layout_width="match_parent"
        android:layout_height="match_parent"
        android:id="@+id/list_view" />

</RelativeLayout>
```

There is nothing particularly interesting about declaring a *ListView* in XML, and because *ListView* can be scrolled automatically, a *ScrollView* is not needed.

The code for adding items to this *ListView* is almost exactly the same as when list navigation was used. Furthermore, the *onItemClickListener* behaves almost exactly the same as the *onNavigationListener*.

```
public class MainActivity extends Activity {

    private Context mContext;

    @Override
    protected void onCreate(Bundle savedInstanceState) {
        super.onCreate(savedInstanceState);
        setContentView(R.layout.activity_main);

        mContext = this;
```

```
    //This ArrayList will hold the text
    //for the list items
    ArrayList<String> listItems =
            new ArrayList<String>();

    //Add items to the list
    for(int i = 0; i < 10; i++){
        listItems.add("Item "+i);
    }

    //Create an ArrayAdapter for the
    //ListView
    ArrayAdapter<String> listAdapter =
            new ArrayAdapter<String>
                (this,android.R.layout.simple_list_item_1,  listItems);

    //Find the ListView
    ListView list = (ListView) findViewById(R.id.list_view);

    //Set the adapter
    list.setAdapter(listAdapter);

    //On item click listener
    list.setOnItemClickListener(new OnItemClickListener() {
        @Override
        public void onItemClick(AdapterView<?> parent, View view,
                                                    int position,long id) {
            //Here the item clicked can be determined
            //from the position (index) of the item clicked

            //A toast is used for example purposes
            //Toasts are useful for debugging
            //information to the screen
            Toast.makeText(mContext, "Item "+position+" was clicked",
                                                    Toast.LENGTH_SHORT);

        }
    });


}

@Override
public boolean onCreateOptionsMenu(Menu menu) {
    // Inflate the menu; this adds items to the action bar if it is
present.
    getMenuInflater().inflate(R.menu.activity_main, menu);
    return true;
```

```
    }
}
```

Note than in *onItemClick* in the anonymous *OnItemClickListener* class, a *Toast* is used. Users of Android will probably recognize *Toasts*, as they are often used to display short notifications while a user is in an application. *Toasts* are also useful for debugging. To show a *Toast*, simply call *makeText* and pass in the application *Context*, the text to display, and the duration the *Toast* should be displayed (uses constants *Toast.LENGTH_SHORT* or *Toast.LENGTH_LONG*).

Here is what happens when "Item 5" is clicked:

In the future when using *ListViews*, something more reasonable will occur when an item is clicked, but for now, simply showing which item was clicked shows how to use *onItemClickedListener*.

6.6.2 Implementing GridView

It is very simple to switch from *ListView* to *GridView*. In the XML layout, simply change the *ListView* to a *GridView* and tell the *GridView* to automatically fit the number of columns.

```
<RelativeLayout
xmlns:android="http://schemas.android.com/apk/res/android"
    xmlns:tools="http://schemas.android.com/tools"
    android:layout_width="match_parent"
    android:layout_height="match_parent"
    tools:context=".MainActivity" >

    <GridView
        android:layout_width="match_parent"
        android:layout_height="match_parent"
        android:id="@+id/grid_view"
        android:numColumns="auto_fit" />

</RelativeLayout>
```

Now in the Java source, change the type of "list" to a *GridView*. It is also a good idea to rename "list" to something more appropriate, such as "grid". There is nothing else needed to switch from *ListView* to *GridView*. Because it is very eas;y to change between these two views when designing an application, it is common to try both and see which fits better. It is also common to use *ListView* on phones and *GridView* on tablets to fill the larger screen.

6.7 Fragment Example

Now that we have covered *Fragments* and *ListViews*, it is time to reveal the power of *Fragments* when designing an application with both phones and tab-

lets in mind. When *Fragments* were introduced into Android, they were originally intended to help developers create applications (and port existing applications) with tablets in mind.

The example app that will used to demonstrate cross compatibility between
different screen sizes has two *Fragments*: one displays a list of items, and one
displays details for an item.

On a device with a small screen, each *Fragment* will be shown one at a time.
First the list *Fragment* will be shown. Upon clicking an item, the item details
Fragment will occupy the entire screen.

On devices with larger screens, the list *Fragment* will be shown as a pane on
the left third of the screen. Upon clicking an item in the list, an item details
Fragment will occupy the right two-thirds of the screen.

To keep this example simple, the *TextFragment* class written earlier will
serve to display an item's details. *ListFragment* will be introduced, which helps
when making *Fragments* exclusively for displaying lists of things. Furthermore,
this is the first project in this book to make use of specifying different layouts
for different screen sizes.

Before diving into the source of the application, here are images of the final
product. On a tablet:

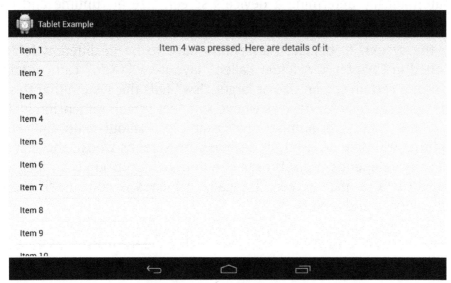

On a phone:

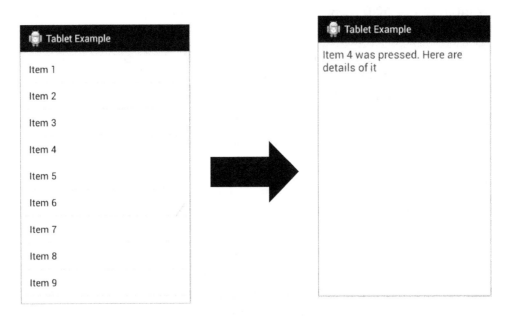

The first step is to create an XML layout for this application. On a tablet, the layout should have two *FrameLayout*s side by side, but on a handset there should only be one *FrameLayout* filling the whole screen. Fortunately, Android can automatically determine a device's screen size at runtime and pick an appropriate layout.

For the system to decide, the layouts have to be in different folders, as mentioned in Chapter 3. A folder called "layout-swXXXdp" can contain XML layouts for a certain screen size or larger. "sw" tells the system that this folder contains layouts only for devices whose smallest screen dimension is XXX dp large, where XXX is a number. For example, "layout-sw600dp" contains layouts that will only be used on devices with screens whose shortest side is 600 density independent pixels or larger. In practice, 600dp is a 7 inch screen, and 720dp is a 10 inch screen. Typically, 7 inches is considered the cutoff between phones and tablets.

At runtime, if the device does not meet the criteria for any of the *layout-swXXXdp* folders, the layout will be retreived from the generic *layout* folder.

The *res* folder for this project should look like the one shown below:

- res
  - drawable-hdpi
  - drawable-ldpi
  - drawable-mdpi
  - drawable-xhdpi
  - layout
    - fragment_container_layout.xml
    - text_fragment.xml
  - layout-sw600dp
    - fragment_container_layout.xml
  - menu
  - values
  - values-v11
  - values-v14

In this project, *text_fragment.xml* was taken from the *TextFragment* example, and *fragment_container_layout.xml* will be the main layout.

In the *layout* version of *fragment_container_layout.xml*, there should only be one *FrameLayout*, because this layout targets phone-sized screens. The source is shown below:

```
<?xml version="1.0" encoding="utf-8"?>
<FrameLayout xmlns:android="http://schemas.android.com/apk/res/android"
    android:id="@+id/container_left"
    android:layout_width="match_parent"
    android:layout_height="match_parent"
    android:layout_margin="8dp" >

</FrameLayout>
```

There is not much that is special to note about this layout, with the exception that *layout_margin* is defined. It is always good to declare at least some margin on each side of a layout for aesthetic reasons. Margins will stop the *FrameLayout* from being immediately adjacent to the screen (and having text inside of the *FrameLayout* touching the edges of the screen).

Pay attention to the *id* of the *FrameLayout*: *container_left*. This name may not make sense now, but later when discussing the Java code, you will see the reason for this naming convention.

For the *layout-sw600dp* version of the layout, use the following source:

```xml
<?xml version="1.0" encoding="utf-8"?>
<LinearLayout xmlns:android="http://schemas.android.com/apk/res/android"
    android:layout_width="match_parent"
    android:layout_height="match_parent"
    android:orientation="horizontal"
    android:layout_marginLeft="16dp"
    android:layout_marginRight="16dp" >

    <FrameLayout
        android:layout_width="0dp"
        android:layout_height="match_parent"
        android:id="@+id/container_left"
        android:layout_weight="1"
        android:layout_marginRight="4dp"
        android:layout_marginTop="4dp"
        android:layout_marginBottom="4dp"
        />

    <FrameLayout
        android:layout_width="0dp"
        android:layout_height="match_parent"
        android:id="@+id/container_right"
        android:layout_weight="2"
        android:layout_margin="8dp"
        />
</LinearLayout>
```

This layout is a little more complicated. First of all, on tablets, it is more visually pleasing to have larger margins, which is why *16dp* is used instead of *8dp*. Next, the two *FrameLayout*s each have weights so that the first *FrameLay-*

out occupies the left third of the screen and the second occupies the right two thirds.

Again, note the *id* names. There is another *container_left* and a *container_right*.

The source for the *TextFragment* is the same as shown before, so it will not be reprinted here.

The code becomes interesting when the source for this application's implementation of *ListFragment* is shown:

```
public class ItemListFragment extends ListFragment{

  public interface ItemListFragmentListener{
    public void onItemSelected(String item);
  }

  String[] items = new String[] {
          "Item 1",
          "Item 2",
          "Item 3",
          "Item 4",
          "Item 5",
          "Item 6",
          "Item 7",
          "Item 8",
          "Item 9",
          "Item 10"
      };

  private ItemListFragmentListener listener;

  public ItemListFragment(){
    listener = null;
  }

  public ItemListFragment(ItemListFragmentListener lis){
    listener = lis;
  }

    @Override
    public View onCreateView(LayoutInflater inflater,
                      ViewGroup container,
```

```
                              Bundle savedInstanceState) {

    //Create an ArrayAdapter
    ArrayAdapter<String> adapter
                       = new ArrayAdapter<String>(
                               inflater.getContext(),
                               android.R.layout.simple_list_item_1,
                               items);

        //Set the list adapter to display the data
        setListAdapter(adapter);

        return super.onCreateView(inflater, container,
                                          savedInstanceState);
    }

    @Override
    public void onListItemClick(ListView l, View view, int position,
                                                     long id) {

        TextView textView = (TextView) view;
        String text = (String) textView.getText();

        if(listener != null){
            listener.onItemSelected(text);
        }
    }
}
```

The first outstanding piece of code is the interface defined within *ItemList-Fragment*. *ItemListFragmentListener* will serve to communicate back to the *Activity* when an item is clicked. In essence, this interface will serve as a *Listener* for the *ItemListFragment*. In this application, the main *Activity* will contain the *Listener* that will either replace the current *Fragment* in view, or will show a *Fragment* in the right hand pane.

In *onCreateView*, an *ArrayAdapter* is created and is set. Next, note that it is not necessary to inflate a *View* explicitly, as returning *super.onCreateView* will return *ListFragment*'s default list layout.

ListFragment has a method called *onListItemClick*, which is called whenever an item is clicked. This method functions exactly the same as *ListView*'s *onItemClick*. In *onListItemClick*, the text of the *View* that was clicked is retrieved. Then, the *ItemListFragmentListener* has its *onItemSelected* method called (provided that the listener is not null).

Here is the code for the *MainActivity*:

```
public class MainActivity extends Activity implements
                                        ItemListFragmentListener {

    private boolean isTablet = false;
    private FrameLayout frameLeft;
    private FrameLayout frameRight;
    private Context mContext;


    @Override
    protected void onCreate(Bundle savedInstanceState) {
        super.onCreate(savedInstanceState);

        setContentView(R.layout.fragment_container_layout);

        mContext = this;

        frameLeft = (FrameLayout) findViewById(R.id.container_left);
        frameRight = (FrameLayout) findViewById(R.id.container_right);

        //frameRight will be null if this is not run on a tablet
        //because findViewById(R.id.container_right) will not
        //be able to find container_right
        if(frameRight != null){
            isTablet = true;
        }

        getFragmentManager()
            .beginTransaction()
            .replace(R.id.container_left, new ItemListFragment(this))
            .commit();

    }

    @Override
    public void onItemSelected(String item) {
```

```
    if(isTablet){  //Check if this is run on a tablet
      //This is a tablet,
      //Put the details on the right pane

      //Create a TextFragment with the
      //appropriate text
      TextFragment details = new TextFragment();
      Bundle args = new Bundle();
      args.putString("text", item + " was pressed."+
                                    " Here are details of it");
      details.setArguments(args);

      //Put the TextFragment into the
      //container on the right
      getFragmentManager()
         .beginTransaction()
         .replace(R.id.container_right, details)
         .commit();
    }else{
      //This is a phone,
      //Start a new Activity to
      //display the details

      //Create a TextFragment with the
      //appropriate text
      TextFragment details = new TextFragment();
      Bundle args = new Bundle();
      args.putString("text", item + " was pressed."+
                                    " Here are details of it");
      details.setArguments(args);

      //Put the TextFragment into the
      //container on the right,
      //also, add it to the back stack
      //so when the user presses the back button
      //this Fragment will be removed
      //and the ListFragment will be shown
      getFragmentManager()
         .beginTransaction()
         .addToBackStack(null)
         .replace(R.id.container_left, details)
         .commit();
    }
  }
}
```

MainActivity contains the logic of what actions to perform when an item in the *ItemListFragment* is clicked. Because of this, it needs to know whether to display item details as an entire page by itself or to put details in its own pane.

This example determines if it is a tablet (and whether or not to use two panes) by attempting to retrieve *container_right*, which only exists in the tablet layout. *findViewById* will return null if the *View* does not exist in the layout, so if *findViewById* returns null in this case then the device must be a phone (because the right pane does not exist).

MainActivity extends *Activity*, as usual, but it also implements *ItemListFragmentListener*, the class that was defined within *ItemListFragment*. Because *MainActivity* implements *ItemListFragmentListener*, the *onItemSelected* method has to be overrriden.

When an item is clicked, if the device is using the tablet layout, then simply put a *TextFragment* into the right pane. If the device is not a tablet, the procedure is mostly the same, except the *TextFragment* is put into the left pane (on a phone, this is the only pane) and the new *TextFragment* is added to the *backStack*. By adding a *Fragment* to the *backStack*, when a user presses the *back* button, the current *Fragment* is removed, and the prior one is shown. If the new *TextFragment* was not added to the *backstack*, then pressing the *back* button while an item's details were being shown would close the app.

Here is a simple flowchart showing the use of the *backStack*:

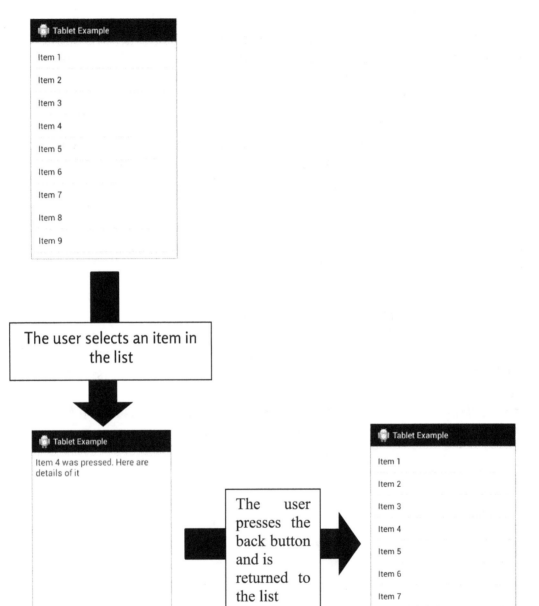

7 Application Life Cycle

7.1 Introduction

Now that most of the various navigation methods have been demonstrated and their implementations have been explained, it is an opportune time to begin understanding the application life cycle. So far, the only life cycle related topic was *Activity* creation, in which *onCreate* was used for setup.

Here, we will talk about the *Intent* system, which allows an Activity to be started and data to be shared. In addition, this chapter will cover when an application is paused, resumed, and stopped, as well as how to deal with orientation changes (screen rotations).

7.2 Intents Explained

*Intent*s are one of the most powerful features. Put simply, an *Intent* is a call to the Android system to perform an action. *Intent*s have a few distinct uses: they can start an *Activity*, start a *Service*, or share data (with or without a specific purpose in mind).

Until now, when showing different screens of an application, *Fragment*s have been added to the *backStack* and replace the prior *Fragment*. Now, you will see how to start a new *Activity* for showing data on a separate screen of an application.

Sharing data showcases the robust nature of *Intent*s. In most other operating systems, sharing data has to be hardcoded. In other words, a "share" button would have to have various social networks, email, and text messaging pre-defined.

Consider a "share" button, as mentioned prior. Say that this button shares text (whether it is a link or data). In order to accomplish this in Android, a new *Intent* has to be created with the text and a flag that limits applications to those that share or send text. Once the *Intent* is started, a list of all applications that can accept text and send or share text will be automatically shown. Once a user selects which application to use, that application receives the data (in a way similar to how arguments work with *Fragment*s) and takes over for the time being.

Any file format or kind of data can be shared with *Intent*s. Examples include phone numbers (that can be opened in the dialer or messaging applications), coordinates (for maps), website addresses (can be opened in a web browser), a song (opened in media players), etc.

*Intent*s can also be used to start specific kinds of applications and receive data from those apps. For example, the camera application can be opened and return a picture taken by the user, or the gallery application could be opened and allow the user to select a picture.

7.3   Starting Specific Activities

Although in the past, *backStack* was used with *Fragment*s to create different screens for an app, the more common method is to create different *Activities* and use the *Intent* system to switch between them.

Starting an *Activity* with an *Intent* is rather easy. The first step will be to create two XML Layouts. Let one of them contain a *TextView* and a *TextView* stating "This is Activity 1." Then create another XML Layout that only contains a *TextView* stating "This is Activity 2."

Here is a sample first layout:

```
<RelativeLayout
xmlns:android="http://schemas.android.com/apk/res/android"
    xmlns:tools="http://schemas.android.com/tools"
    android:layout_width="match_parent"
    android:layout_height="match_parent"
    tools:context=".MainActivity" >

    <TextView
        android:id="@+id/text1"
        android:layout_width="wrap_content"
        android:layout_height="wrap_content"
        android:layout_centerHorizontal="true"
        android:layout_centerVertical="true"
        android:text="This is Activity 1" />

    <Button
        android:id="@+id/first_activity_button"
        android:layout_width="wrap_content"
        android:layout_height="wrap_content"
        android:layout_below="@id/text1"
        android:layout_centerHorizontal="true"
        android:text="Go to the second Activity" />

</RelativeLayout>
And here is a sample second layout:
<RelativeLayout
xmlns:android="http://schemas.android.com/apk/res/android"
    xmlns:tools="http://schemas.android.com/tools"
    android:layout_width="match_parent"
```

```
    android:layout_height="match_parent"
    tools:context=".MainActivity" >

    <TextView
        android:id="@+id/text2"
        android:layout_width="wrap_content"
        android:layout_height="wrap_content"
        android:layout_centerHorizontal="true"
        android:layout_centerVertical="true"
        android:text="This is Activity 2" />

</RelativeLayout>
```

Now it is time to create a new *Activity*. As mentioned in the second chapter, an *Activity* has to be declared in the *AndroidManifest*, as well as in Java. Fortunately, the Android Development Tools will do all this automatically if a specific dialog is used.

Right click on *src*, navigate to *New* and then *Other...*

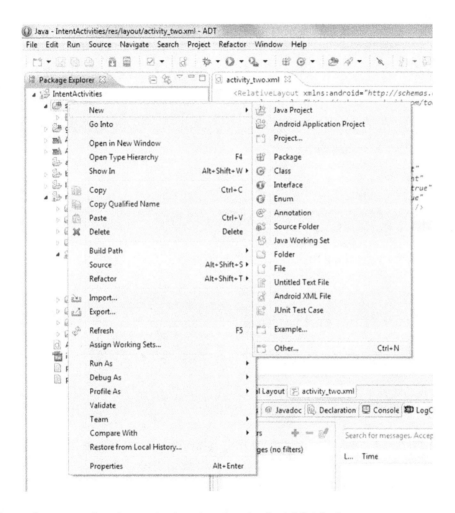

Then chose *Android Activity* (under the *Android* folder)

Upon clicking *Next*, the same dialog is shown from when this project was created. Chose *BlankActivity*. As for the name of the *Activity*, call it something appropriate, such as "SecondaryActivity." Click *Finish*.

This dialog should have created a new Java source file, an XML file, and declared the *Activity* in *AndroidManifest.xml*. Delete the XML file that was created, as the second layout was already created. Change the new *Activity*'s Java source to set the second layout as the content view.

The *MainActivity* will set the content view to the first layout (with the button). Then the button's *onClickListener* will create and execute a new *Intent* to start the second *Activity*.

MainActivity's code should look similar to this:

```
public class MainActivity extends Activity {
   Context mContext;

   @Override
   protected void onCreate(Bundle savedInstanceState) {
      super.onCreate(savedInstanceState);
      setContentView(R.layout.activity_one);

      mContext = this;

      Button b = (Button) findViewById(R.id.first_activity_button);
      b.setOnClickListener(new OnClickListener() {
         @Override
         public void onClick(View v) {
            //Create a new Intent
            Intent i = new Intent(mContext, SecondaryActivity.class);
            //Start the Intent
            mContext.startActivity(i);
         }
      });
   }

   @Override
   public boolean onCreateOptionsMenu(Menu menu) {
      // Inflate the menu;
      //this adds items to the
      //action bar if it is present.
      getMenuInflater().inflate(R.menu.activity_main, menu);
      return true;
   }

}
```

Note the arguments when creating an *Intent* to start a specific *Activity*. The first argument is simply the *Context* from which the *Activity* will be launched from, and the second is the *class* property of the *Activity* to be launched. In short, the *class* property in Java is a way to refer to a class instead of a specific object. In this case, the *class* is passed in because the system (not this app) will be creating an instance of the new *Activity*.

This kind of *Intent* is commonly referred to as an *Explicit Intent*, because it explicitly states which *Activity* should be launched.

Try running the application. When the button is clicked, the second *Activity* is launched. When the "back" button is pressed, the second *Activity* is closed and the first *Activity* is visible again.

7.4 Implementing the Up Button

By default, the "back" button calls *finish* on the visible *Activity*. *finish* is used to close an *Activity* (the equivalent of *System.exit* in normal Java). A relatively new design standard is the addition of an "Up" icon in the *ActionBar* when it is possible to return to a "higher" (as in higher on the hierarchy of pages) page. When the icon is clicked, the currently shown *Activity* should be closed (with a call to *finish*) and the previously shown *Activity* should be visible.

Here is what the second *Activity* looks like without the "Up" arrow:

This is how the second *Activity* appears with the "Up" arrow:

The following source shows how to implement this design custom.

In *onCreate* of the second *Activity*, the following code shows the "Up" icon and makes it clickable:

```
//Get the instance of ActionBar
ActionBar actionBar = getActionBar();

//Display the "back" arrow on
//the app icon in the upper left
//of the ActionBar
actionBar.setDisplayHomeAsUpEnabled(true);

//Allow the ActionBar app icon
//to be clicked
actionBar.setHomeButtonEnabled(true);
```

Now that the icon is shown and can be clicked, the *Activity* has to *finish* when the icon is clicked. The "Up" button does not have an *onClickListener*; instead it behaves like a *MenuItem*.

The icon has an ID of *android.R.id.home*. The following code shows how to receive when the "Up" icon is pressed and *finish* the *Activity*.

```
@Override
public boolean onMenuItemSelected(int featureId, MenuItem item) {
   switch(item.getItemId()){
   case android.R.id.home:
     //The "Up" icon was clicked

     //Call finish() to close this Activity
     finish();
     return true;
   }
   return false;
}
```

This code should seem familiar from the discussion of *ActionBar*. Try putting this code into the second *Activity* and run the application.

7.5 Sharing Data

Sharing data to other application is one of the most common features of an application. A news reader application should be able to share articles, a storefront app might be able to share product listings, and even an e-book reading application should be able to share what the user is reading to social networks. Thankfully, *Intents* make sharing data easy.

The kinds of *Intents* used in this example are *Implicit Intents*. Unlike *Explicit Intents*, an *Activity* is never specified. Instead, with *Implicit Intents*, the Android system decides which *Activity* or *Activities* are suitable for the data being passed in.

To make matters simple, this example has many *MenuItems* in the *Action-Bar*, each of which will execute a unique intent that demonstrates a different action.

Upon tapping "Text," the text messaging or email application can be chosen. By tapping "Phone," the dialer will be shown with the phone number "888-555-2222" already entered. When "URL" is selected, the web browser opens and navigates to google.com. Note that if the device has multiple applications that can handle an *Intent* (for example email and text messaging), then a dialog is presented that allows the user to choose among them.

Here is the code for *onMenuItemSelected*:

```
@Override
  public boolean onMenuItemSelected(int featureId, MenuItem item) {
    switch(item.getItemId()){
    case R.id.menu_text:
      //Share some text
```

```
        Intent textIntent = new Intent();
        //This intent should be directed only
        //at Activities that send data
        textIntent.setAction(Intent.ACTION_SEND);
        //Put the text into this intent
        textIntent.putExtra(Intent.EXTRA_TEXT, "This is some text");
        //This intent shares plain text
        textIntent.setType("text/plain");
        //Start the Activity, the system will
        //display a dialog to choose which application
        //to use
        startActivity(Intent.createChooser(textIntent, "Send with"));
        return true;
    case R.id.menu_phone:
        Intent phoneIntent = new Intent();
        phoneIntent.setAction(Intent.ACTION_DIAL);
        //This intent uses Uri to parse a more human
        //readable command
        String phoneString = "tel:" + "888-555-2222";
        phoneIntent.setData(Uri.parse(phoneString));
        startActivity(Intent.createChooser(phoneIntent, "Dial with"));
        return true;
    case R.id.menu_url:
        Intent urlIntent = new Intent();
        urlIntent.setAction(Intent.ACTION_VIEW);
        //Uri can also parse URLs
        String urlString = "http://www.google.com";
        urlIntent.setData(Uri.parse(urlString));
        startActivity(Intent.createChooser(urlIntent, "Open with"));
        return true;
    }
    return false;
}
```

The first part of each of these *Intent*s is the action to perform. *Intent* has many static *String*s for possible actions. This example shows three of them: *ACTION_SEND*, *ACTION_DIAL*, and *ACTION_VIEW*. Others actions include *ACTION_EDIT*, *ACTION_PICK*, and *ACTION_SEARCH*.

There are two different ways to put data into an *Intent*. The first is shown by the *menu_text* case. The *putExtra* method is similar to the methods in *Bundle*. *Intent.EXTRA_TEXT* is a static *String*. Other types of extras include *In-*

tent.EXTRA_EMAIL (email addresses), *Intent.EXTRA_SUBJECT* (subject of an email) and *Intent.EXTRA_HTML_TEXT* (plain text that should be interpreted as HTML), as well as other more exotic types of extras. Multiple extras can be put into a single *Intent* (for example, *EXTRA_TEXT*, *EXTRA_EMAIL*, and *EXTRA_SUBJECT* could all be used together).

If *putExtra* is being used, it is necessary to set the type of the data. The string passed in *"text/plain"* is known as a MIME type. MIME types are not exclusive to Android. MIME is a specification for describing files that was originally used on the internet. Android will accept all of the common MIME types; the table below shows the most common Android accepted MIME types:

Mime Type	File Type
text/plain	.txt, .c, .h, .java
text/xml	.xml
text/html	.html, .htm
text/richtext	.rtf, .rtx
audio/mpeg	.mpa, .mpg, .mp2
video/mpeg	.m1v, .mp2v, .
video/avi	.avi
audio/wav	.wav
audio/mpeg3	.mp3
image/gif	.gif
image/jpeg	.jpg, .jpeg
image/png	.png
image/bmp	.bmp
application/pdf	.pdf

application/msword	.doc
application/excel	.xlc

After setting the desired action, data, and MIME type of the data, the *Intent* can be executed with *startActivity*. Just like before, when the *Activity* to launch was specified, a new *Activity* will be started.

By using *Intent.createChooser*, if multiple *Activity*s can accept the MIME type and perform the action specified, a list will appear for the user to choose from. If there is only one *Activity* that can accept the data, the chooser dialog will never appear. The arguments of *Intent.createChooser* are an *Implicit Intent* and a *String* for the title of the chooser dialog box.

The other means of setting data for an *Intent* is through the *Uri* class. A *Uri* is simply a link to data. Like with MIME types, there are a few different *Uri* types. In this example, *tel* in combination with a number tells the system that this is a phone number. A website or file address can also be passed in. By using *Uri.parse*, the data type is determined by the system, so *setType* should not be used in conjunction with *Uri.parse*.

Try running this application and pressing all of the *MenuItems*. Each should open an appropriate application and display the data.

After selecting "Text":   After selecting "Phone":

7.6   Basic Lifecycle

In the second chapter, *onCreate* was briefly mentioned, along with *onPause*, *onResume*, and other lifecycle methods. These methods are called by the system exclusively; an application can never call its own *onCreate* method. Here is a brief description of when each of the lifecycle methods is executed.

Method	Meaning
onCreate	The application was launched or the screen was rotated. After *onCreate*, *onStart* will be called
onPause	The *Activity* is underneath another *Activity*

onStop	The *Activity* is no longer visible and cannot be accessed by pressing the "back" button. The *Activity* can now either be restarted or destroyed
onDestroy	*finish* is called from the app or the system
onResume	The *Activity* is visible again directly after *onPause* was called or after any call of *onStart*
onStart	The *Activity* is restarted immediately following a call to *onRestart* or *onCreate* has finished

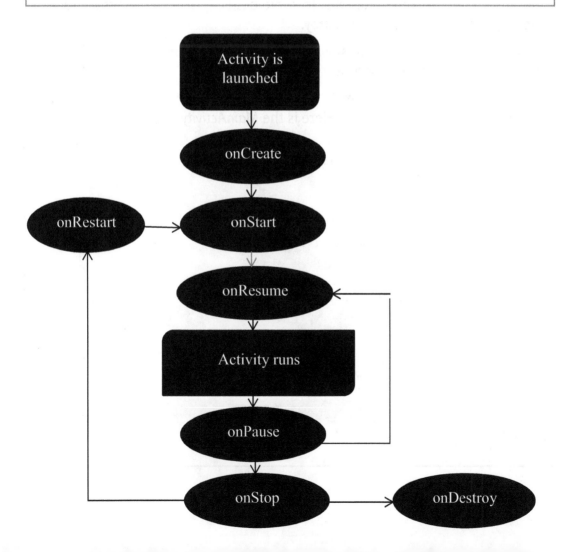

One important nuance to note is that *onPause, onStop, onDestroy,* and *onCreate* are called (in that order, followed by *onStart* and *onResume,* as always) when screen orientation changes. This means that when the screen rotates, information about the current views can be lost. In the prior example applications, when rotating the screen, the state would be lost. For example, *EditText View*s would lose any text that was entered into them.

There are steps that can be taken to save an application's state (both across restarts of the application and screen rotations) that will be demonstrated in this chapter. In general, the means to keep data involves overriding *onPause* and *onResume.* In some cases, it may be necessary to also override *onStart, onStop,* or *onDestroy.*

Before implementing state-saving code, it is necessary to have an intuitive feel of which lifecycle methods are called when.

This small sample program is based off of a blank project and displays *Toast*s in each life cycle method. Here is the *MainActivity.java* file's contents:

```java
public class MainActivity extends Activity {
   Context mContext;

   @Override
   protected void onCreate(Bundle savedInstanceState) {
      super.onCreate(savedInstanceState);
      setContentView(R.layout.activity_main);

      mContext = this;

      Toast.makeText(this, "onCreate", Toast.LENGTH_SHORT).show();
   }

   @Override
   protected void onDestroy() {
      super.onDestroy();
      Toast.makeText(this, "onDestroy", Toast.LENGTH_SHORT).show();
   }

   @Override
   protected void onPause() {
      super.onPause();
```

```
        Toast.makeText(this, "onPause", Toast.LENGTH_SHORT).show();
    }

    @Override
    protected void onRestart() {
        super.onRestart();
        Toast.makeText(this, "onRestart", Toast.LENGTH_SHORT).show();

    }

    @Override
    protected void onResume() {
        super.onResume();
        Toast.makeText(this, "onResume",
                Toast.LENGTH_SHORT).show();
    }

    @Override
    protected void onStart() {
        super.onStart();
        Toast.makeText(this, "onStart",
                Toast.LENGTH_SHORT).show();
    }

    @Override
    protected void onStop() {
        super.onStop();
        Toast.makeText(this, "onStop", Toast.LENGTH_SHORT).show();
    }
}
```

Try opening and closing the application (both by pressing the "back" button and the "home" button), and rotating the screen (on the emulator, use the number pad buttons 7 and 9, with Num Lock enabled). Note that pressing the "back" button to exit calls *onDestroy* in addition to *onPause* and *onStop* that are called when the "home" button is pressed.

Create a new project. In the *activity_main.xml*, create a new *EditText*, like so:

```
<RelativeLayout
xmlns:android="http://schemas.android.com/apk/res/android"
    xmlns:tools="http://schemas.android.com/tools"
```

```
        android:layout_width="match_parent"
        android:layout_height="match_parent"
        tools:context=".MainActivity" >

        <EditText
            android:id="@+id/text_input"
            android:layout_margin="24dp"
            android:layout_width="match_parent"
            android:layout_height="wrap_content"
            android:layout_centerHorizontal="true"
            android:layout_centerVertical="true" />

</RelativeLayout>
```

Run the application. Enter some text into the *EditText*, then rotate the screen or leave the application (with the "home" button) and re-open it. The text in the *EditText* will be gone.

There are two additional lifecycle methods that have not been disclosed yet: *onSaveInstanceState* and *onRestoreInstanceState*. These two methods provide temporary storage useful for keeping the status of the user interface across application rotations, pauses, and stops. This is not a way to persistently store data, if *onDestroy* is called, this data will be lost.

It may have been a mystery in the past why *onCreate* has a *Bundle* as an argument. In short, this *Bundle* is the same one that can be written to and read from in *onSaveInstanceState* and *onRestoreInstanceState*. *Bundles* should be familiar by now, so there is not a need for too much explanation.

```
public class MainActivity extends Activity {

    EditText textInput;

    @Override
    protected void onCreate(Bundle savedInstanceState) {
        super.onCreate(savedInstanceState);
        setContentView(R.layout.activity_main);

        textInput = (EditText) findViewById(R.id.text_input);
```

```
    if(savedInstanceState 1= null &&
                savedInstanceState.containsKey("text_input")) {
      textInput.setText( savedInstanceState.getString("text_input") );
    }

  }

  @Override
  protected void onSaveInstanceState(Bundle outState) {
    super.onSaveInstanceState(outState);
    outState.putString("text_input", textInput.getText().toString());
  }
}
```

onSaveInstanceState is called before *onStop*, but may be before or after *on-Pause*. *onRestoreInstanceState* is called after *onCreate*, but may be called before or after *onStart*. In any case, it is typical to save the application's state in *on-SaveInstanceState* and restore state at the end of *onCreate*.

How to save state is shown in the above code. In *onSaveInstanceState*, the text entered into the *EditText*'s text is saved with the key *"text_input"*. In *onCreate*, if *savedInstanceState* is not null and contains the key *"text_input"*, then the *EditText*'s text is set to what was saved.

Try running the application. Enter some text and then rotate the screen. The *EditText* should still have the text that was entered into it. Also, try pressing the "home" button and reopening the application. The text should still be saved. Note that if the "back" button is pressed, *onDestroy* will be called, so the *savedInstanceState Bundle* will be destroyed, and the text will not be restored if the application relaunches.

Before rotating:

After rotating:

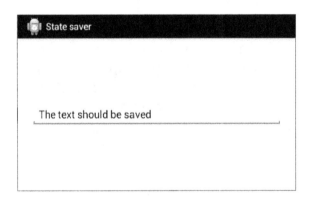

Every *Activity* in an application should be able to save information about its user interface and restore it when the app is resumed or restarted. This is something every user expects in an application, especially with recent releases of Android, where true multitasking and quick application switching have become a highly touted feature over other mobile platforms.

8 Multithreading and Performance Optimization

8.1 Introduction

To a user, there is nothing more frustrating than an unresponsive interface. Therefore, performing lengthy commands on the main thread of an application is a bad idea, as it can lead to stutters, dropped frames, or in the worst case scenario, the "App not responding" dialog appearing.

It is imperative than any operation that may take more than a few milliseconds should be put into a separate thread in order to allow the interface thread to continue responding to screen touches, rotation changes, and other interactions. Any process that involves reading or writing files, getting images from resources, and especially network operations should be on a separate thread.

Every application should be able to update the display at sixty times (frames) per second, which means that each frame can take at most 16.6 milliseconds. It is typical for the layout to take around five milliseconds to draw, which leaves 11.6 milliseconds for an application's computations. Therefore it is best to keep computations to five milliseconds or less, which allows for a comfortable amount of extra time left.

Five milliseconds may seem to be plenty of time for most operations. In practice, setting up the entire interface with *onClickListeners* takes only a few milliseconds. However, anytime there is a file being read, there is latency between 1 and 5 milliseconds or even higher[4], which almost guarantees that at least one frame will have to be skipped. Using multiple threads solves this.

Other ways of optimizing performance include simplifying the hierarchies of layouts and reducing overdraw, both of which will be covered.

8.2 Example Without Multithreading

A good time to use multithreading is when loading an image. To demonstrate why, this example loads a large image and displays it.

Here is the layout file, which contains a *Button* and an *ImageView*:

```
<LinearLayout xmlns:android="http://schemas.android.com/apk/res/android"
    xmlns:tools="http://schemas.android.com/tools"
    android:layout_width="match_parent"
    android:layout_height="match_parent"
    tools:context=".MainActivity"
    android:orientation="vertical" >

    <Button
        android:id="@+id/load_image_button"
        android:layout_width="wrap_content"
        android:layout_height="wrap_content"
        android:text="Load Image"
        />

    <ImageView
        android:id="@+id/image_frame"
        android:layout_width="match_parent"
        android:layout_height="0dp"
        android:layout_weight="1"
        />

</LinearLayout>
```

---

[4] This assumes the device is using a NAND flash disk, which is typical. Latency when performing writes can be longer than 5 milliseconds.

In this application, an image will be loaded when the button is pressed. In addition, the time it takes to load the image will be written to the console. Once the button is pressed, it will disappear.

The Java code for the *MainActivity* should look similar to this:

```
public class MainActivity extends Activity {
  Button mLoadButton;
  ImageView mImageframe;

  @Override
  protected void onCreate(Bundle savedInstanceState) {
    super.onCreate(savedInstanceState);
    setContentView(R.layout.activity_main);

    mImageframe = (ImageView) findViewById(R.id.image_frame);

    mLoadButton = (Button) findViewById(R.id.load_image_button);

    mLoadButton.setOnClickListener(new OnClickListener(){
      @Override
      public void onClick(View v) {
        long startTime = System.currentTimeMillis();

        mImageframe.setImageResource(R.drawable.space);

        long time = System.currentTimeMillis()
                                    - startTime;

        Log.d("MainActivity","Time to load: "
                        + time + " milliseconds");
      }
    });
  }

}
```

R.drawable.space refers to an image that was taken from NASA. For the purposes of this example, any image will work, but the effect is best seen when the image is large (larger than 2000 by 2000 pixels).

Run the application and press the button. If the app is being run on an emulator, expect a significant delay between the time the button is pressed and when the image appears. Even on a device, there is a noticeable pause.

Note that after the button is touched, it still is drawn as highlighted until the image is displayed. This is because the image loading process is being run in the main thread, which also draws screen updates.

Upon checking the logcat output, it can be seen that the stutter while loading the image is unacceptable.

```
MainActivity    Time to load: 1261 milliseconds
```

If the version of Android being run on the emulator or device is 4.1 or higher, a message from *Choreographer* will also appear. *Choreographer* was created to diagnose performance issues and will write to the log whenever one or more frames are skipped.

```
Choreographer   Skipped 73 frames!  The application may be doing too much work on i
                ts main thread.
```

8.3 Basic Multithreading with Runnable

This time, instead of loading the image in the main thread, a *Runnable* will be used. *Runnable* is a standard Java class and is not Android specific. *Runnable* is an abstract class with one method: *run*. All the computation that a *Runnable* does should be written in *run*.

Here is the above code adapted to use a *Runnable* to load the image:

```java
public class MainActivity extends Activity {
   Context mContext;
   Button mLoadButton;
   ImageView mImageframe;

   Bitmap image;

   @Override
```

```java
protected void onCreate(Bundle savedInstanceState) {
    super.onCreate(savedInstanceState);
    setContentView(R.layout.activity_main);

    mContext = this;

    mImageframe = (ImageView) findViewById(R.id.image_frame);

    mLoadButton = (Button) findViewById(R.id.load_image_button);
    mLoadButton.setOnClickListener(new OnClickListener(){
        @Override
        public void onClick(View v) {

            Runnable r = new Runnable(){
                @Override
                public void run(){
                        long startTime = System.currentTimeMillis();

                        if(image != null){
                                image.recycle();
                        }
                        image = BitmapFactory.decodeResource(
                                            mContext.getResources(),
                                            R.drawable.space);


                mImageframe.post(new Runnable(){
                    @Override
                    public void run(){

                mImageframe.setImageBitmap(image);
                    }
                });

                long time = System.currentTimeMillis()

                - startTime;

                Log.d("MainActivity","Time to load: "
                            + time + " milliseconds");
                }
            };

            new Thread(r).start();

        }
```

```
        });
    }

}
```

This code is a little more complicated than the previous example. Part of this complexity comes from an Android limitation where the user interface can only be modified on the main thread. This means that instead of using the simpler *setImageResource*, *setImageBitmap* has to be used.

The image has to be decoded into a *Bitmap* on a secondary thread and then the *ImageView* has to have its content set on the main thread. Fortunately, almost all of the computation time used to load the image from memory and decode it into a *Bitmap* object.

The *BitmapFactory* class is capable of decoding resources into *Bitmaps*, as shown. Now the *ImageView* has to be told to display the *Bitmap*. The *post* method (from the *View* class) allows operations to be run on the main thread. The only argument is a *Runnable*, so in this runnable, simply use *setImageBitmap* to set the *ImageView*'s displayed image.

A side note on memory management: because the application is keeping a reference to the *Bitmap*, the system cannot garbage collect memory used by that *Bitmap* until the *Activity* is destroyed. In the case where the button is pressed multiple times, the *recycle* method has to be called on the *Bitmap*, which frees *Bitmap*'s memory.

Try running the application. Upon pressing the button, the button's highlight should disappear almost instantaneously when the button is released. This is because the main thread is not occupied with decoding resources and is able to draw frames.

The logcat output may show that this method takes longer to set the image:

```
MainActivity    Time to load: 1327 milliseconds
```

This is due to the slightly increased overhead when creating *Runnables*. None of the frames should have been skipped (although on slow emulators, there may be a few skipped frames).

8.4   Multithreading with AsyncTask

AsyncTask is an Android specific abstract class specifically designed to run an operation in a separate thread and then make changes to the user interface. It also has support for periodically running code on the main thread for the purpose of publishing progress.

AsyncTask has three primary private methods: doInBackground, onProgressUpdate, and onPostExecute.

doInBackground runs on a separate thread, whereas onProgressUpdate and onPostExecute run on the main thread. This makes it easy to modify the view layout after the background thread finishes without having to use post. For this reason, AsyncTask is the preferred method of multithreading an application.

Some other private methods of an *AsyncTask* include *isCancelled* (unlike a *Runnable*, an *AsyncTask* can be cancelled) and *onPreExecute* (which is also run on the main thread).

AsyncTask makes full use of generics. Here is an example instantiation of an *AsyncTask*:

```
loadImageTask = new AsyncTask<Integer, Float, Boolean>(){
```

In an *AsyncTask*, the generics correspond to arguments and return types of the three main methods. The first generic is type of values passed to *doInBackground*, the second is the type of object passed to *onProgressUpdate*, and the final generic type is the type of the argument of *onPostExecute*.

The first generic type in this *AsyncTask* is an *Integer* (generic types can only have *Object*s) because reference types (like *R.drawable.space* are *int*s). *onPublishProgress* takes a *Float* in this example (because floats are good for percentages). And finally, *onPostExecute* will take a *Boolean* (to determine if the operation was successful or not).

When executing an *AsyncTask*, the *execute* method is called. *execute* can take any number of arguments, the reason for this will be shown when the entire code example is explained.

Here is the same image loading example written with an *AsyncTask* instead of a *Runnable*:

```java
public class MainActivity extends Activity {
    Context mContext;
    Button mLoadButton;
    ImageView mImageframe;

    Bitmap image;


    AsyncTask<Integer, Float, Boolean> loadImageTask = new
                              AsyncTask<Integer, Float, Boolean>(){
        long startTime;

        @Override
        protected void onPreExecute(){
            //Before doing any computation,
            //keep track of the start time for
            //comparison with Runnable and no
            //multithreading.
            startTime = System.currentTimeMillis();
        }

        @Override
        protected Boolean doInBackground(Integer... imageResources) {
            //This example only loads one of
            //the images, so choose the first one

            if(imageResources == null ||
                imageResources.length < 1) {
                //There are no images to load
```

```java
            return false;
        }

        if(isCancelled()){
            //The task was cancelled
            return false;
        }

        if(image != null){
            //Save memory if
            //the image was already
            //loaded
            image.recycle();
        }

        //Load the image
        image = BitmapFactory.decodeResource(
                                mContext.getResources(),
                                imageResources[0]);

        //Update the progress
        //(this will result in
        // onProgressUpdate being
        // called)
        publishProgress(1f);

    //The image was loaded successfully
        return true;
    }

    @Override
    protected void onProgressUpdate(Float... progress){
        //This example is only loading one image,
        //so there is no need to update a
        //progress bar
        Log.d("loadImageTask","Progess: " + (progress[0] * 100) + "%");
    }

    @Override
    protected void onPostExecute(Boolean result){
        if(result){
            //The image was loaded successfully.
            //Set the image frame to display
            //the loaded image
            mImageframe.setImageBitmap(image);
```

```
            //Log out the time it took to display
                long loadTime = System.currentTimeMillis() - startTime;
                Log.d("loadImageTask","Loaded Image successfully");
                Log.d("loadImageTask","Time to load: "+loadTime);
            }else{
                Log.e("loadImageTask", "Problem loading image");
            }
        }

    };

    @Override
    protected void onCreate(Bundle savedInstanceState) {
    super.onCreate(savedInstanceState);
    setContentView(R.layout.activity_main);

    mContext = this;

    mImageframe = (ImageView) findViewById(R.id.image_frame);

    mLoadButton = (Button) findViewById(R.id.load_image_button);
    mLoadButton.setOnClickListener(new OnClickListener(){
        @Override
        public void onClick(View v) {
            //Execute the task with the
            //space image resource as
            //an argument
            loadImageTask.execute(R.drawable.space);
        }
    });
  }

}
```

In this code, *loadImageTask* is defined with an anonymous class in a way similar to defining an *OnClickListener*.

The *onPreExecute* code simply saves the start time of the task's execution.

The *doInBackground* code is where *AsyncTask* becomes interesting. Note the syntax on the arguments. The three periods after the argument type indicates that any number of arguments of that type can be passed in. This is called a "vararg" because there can be a variable number of arguments.

Here is a simpler example of a method that uses a vararg:

```
public int add(int... numbers){
    int sum = 0;

    if(numbers != null){
        for(int i = 0; i < numbers.length; i++){
            sum += numbers[i];
        }
    }

    return sum;
}
```

Functionally, when getting arguments, they appear as an array. The *add* example illustrates this.

Here are some ways the *add* method could be called:

```
int total1 = add(5);
    int total2 = add(2, 4, 5);
    int total3 = add(1, 2);
```

AsyncTask uses varargs to allow any number of data inputs to be worked with. The image loading example only loads the first argument passed in, but the next *AsyncTask* example is written to be able to take multiple arguments.

In *doInBackground*, first check arguments passed in. If there are no arguments, then simply return *false*, which *onPostExecute* will interpret as the operation being unsuccessful. Also, check to see if the task was already cancelled; if so, return *false*.

After decoding the image, progress is published and *true* is returned. This app does not have a progress bar, so all *onProgressUpdate* does is write to logcat. *onPostExecute* interprets the *true* from *doInBackground* to mean that the image was successfully loaded and sets the *ImageView*'s bitmap to display, as well as writing the total elapsed time to logcat.

Run this application, and press the load image button. Then check the log output.

```
loadImageTask    Progess: 100.0%
loadImageTask    Loaded Image successfully
loadImageTask    Time to load: 1365
```

Try pressing the load image button again. The application will crash. Upon checking the log output, the error states that an *AsyncTask* can only be executed once, so if a task has to be repeated, a new instance of that *AsyncTask* has to be created. Note that this differs from a *Runnable*[5].

8.5 Performance Analysis Tools

The Android SDK comes bundled with a few extremely powerful performance analysis tools that allow developers to see how much memory objects are consuming, how much time methods took to execute, how complex a screen layout is, and how much overdraw exists.

These SDK tools exist in the "tools" folder of the Android SDK folder.

8.5.1 Monitor

Monitor is one of the more extensive tools to analyze performance. Open "monitor" in the "tools" folder. Monitor allows easy access to both *DDMS*

---

[5] The underlying mechanics of *AsyncTask* and *Runnable* are the same, however. In Java, when a thread finishes, it is destroyed. When a *Runnable* is run, it is typical to use *new Thread(runnable).start( )*, which creates a new thread for the runnable. An *AsyncTask* is always tied to one thread, so after being run once the thread is destroyed, hence why an *AsyncTask* can only be executed once.

(used to track threads, network usage, and memory allocation) and *Heirarchy View* (which shows the hierarchy of *Views* on the screen).

First, let's examine DDMS. In the top right, be sure that DDMS is selected instead of Hierarchy View. The left pane shows all the connected devices and emulators. Start an emulator or connect a device (if this has not been done already).

Underneath each device is a list of all the running processes (named by their package names). Run the *AsyncTask* multithreaded image example on the device and choose the process in the left-hand pane based on the package name in the manifest.

Monitor, with DDMS selected:

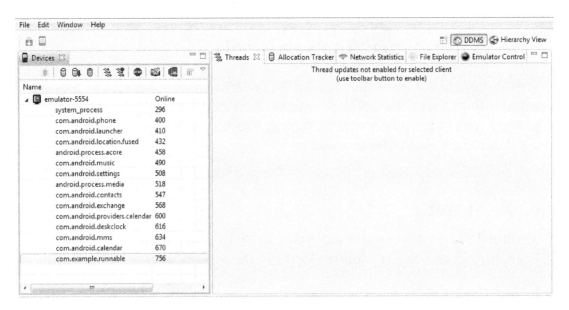

The *AsyncTask* Example App's process selected:

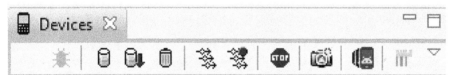

There are ten buttons on the device pane toolbar.

From right to left, they are Debug (ant icon), Update Heap (green cylinder), Dump HPROF File (green cylinder with red arrow), Cause Garbage Collection (garbage can), Update Threads (three arrows), Start Method Profiling (three arrows with stop sign), Stop Process (stop sign), Screen Capture (camera), and Dump View Hierarchy (devices).

8.5.2 **Thread Inspector**

First, threads will be discussed. With the *AsyncTask* example process selected, click the Update Threads button and switch to the Threads tab on the right-hand pane.

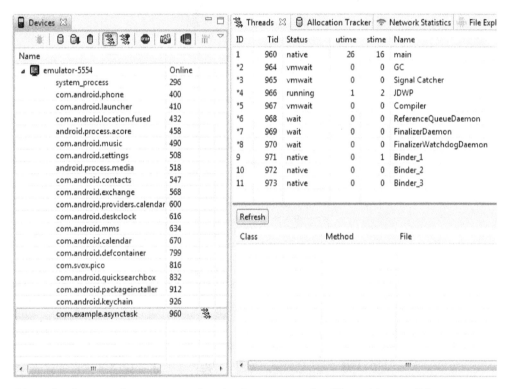

Now, in the emulator or on the device, press the "Load Image" button.

Note that a new thread appears!

ID	Tid	Status	utime	stime	Name
11	1119	wait	104	9	AsyncTask #1

In this view, *utime* is up time, which is the time that the thread has been running the application's code. *stime* is system time, which is the time that the thread ran system code. Earlier when using logcat to time the thread execution, the output stated that the thread took over one second to run, whereas utime is only showing 103. The reason for this disparity is that utime and stime measure in 10 millisecond units (commonly called a "jiffy"), and the application's log output was measured in milliseconds.

The thread monitor tool is useful for determining where most of the processing time occurs (and if too much occurs in the main thread).

8.5.3 Allocation Tracker

The next tool is the Allocation Tracker, which can reveal what an application's memory is being used for. In the Allocation Tracker tab, Press "Start Tracking" and then "Get Allocations". Now all the memory allocations made by the application is displayed.

Here is the first result in that list:

Alloc Order	Allocation Size	Allocated Class	Thread Id	Allocated in	Allocated in
136	8350416	byte[]	11	android.graphics.BitmapFactory	nativeDecodeAsset

This is an 8.35 MB memory allocation made by the *BitmapFactory* class. This makes sense, because the image that was loaded was particularly large. Furthermore, the memory was allocated in thread 11. Check the Threads tab again: AsyncTask #1 has an ID of 11. This proves that the memory was allocated in the *AsyncTask* when decoding the bitmap.

In addition to these inferences, clicking on the allocation will show exactly which methods were called to allocate the memory:

Class	Method	File
android.graphics.BitmapFactory	nativeDecodeAsset	BitmapFactory.java
android.graphics.BitmapFactory	decodeStream	BitmapFactory.java
android.graphics.BitmapFactory	decodeResourceStre...	BitmapFactory.java
android.graphics.BitmapFactory	decodeResource	BitmapFactory.java
android.graphics.BitmapFactory	decodeResource	BitmapFactory.java
com.example.asynctask.MainActivity$1	doInBackground	MainActivity.java
com.example.asynctask.MainActivity$1	doInBackground	MainActivity.java
android.os.AsyncTask$2	call	AsyncTask.java
java.util.concurrent.FutureTask	run	FutureTask.java
android.os.AsyncTask$SerialExecutor$1	run	AsyncTask.java
java.util.concurrent.ThreadPoolExecutor	runWorker	ThreadPoolExecutor.java
java.util.concurrent.ThreadPoolExecut...	run	ThreadPoolExecutor.java
java.lang.Thread	run	Thread.java

Here it can be seen that although the memory was allocated in a method called *nativeDecodeAsset* in *BitmapFactory*, that method was called by *doInBackground* in the *MainActivity* class.

The memory allocation tool is useful to see if an application is being wasteful with memory. In this case, the Image Load Application is being inefficient with memory, because it makes no sense to load a 2000 by 2000 pixel image on a 540 by 960 pixel screen. There are ways to scale the image down to save memory, but that is not important here.

The other tabs in the DDMS are not particularly important to analyzing performance. The networking tab will become useful on applications that connect to the internet. The file explorer allows the internal Android file system to be modified, and the emulator control tab can allow developers to fake calls or incoming text messages, the state of the network connection, and GPS signals.

8.5.4 TraceView

Traceview is one of the most powerful tools included. Traceview allows developers to see which methods take the most processing time and which methods run on which threads.

Close the *AsyncTask* example by using the "back" button (in order for the *Activity* to be destroyed). Open the application again, but do not load the image. In DDMS, press "Start Method Profiling" (in the Devices pane. Load the image in the application by pressing the button; then click "Stop Method Profiling".

After a short delay, the traceview data will appear.

msec: 489.61   max msec: 5,800 (real time, dual clock)

Timeline scale: 0, 1,000, 2,000, 3,000, 4,000, 5,000

Threads:
- [1] main
- [11] AsyncTask #1
- [6] ReferenceQueueDaemon
- [7] FinalizerDaemon
- [2] GC
- [4] JDWP
- [8] FinalizerWatchdogDaemon

Name	Incl Cpu Time %	Incl Cpu Time	Excl Cpu Time %	Excl Cpu Time	Incl Real Time %	Incl Real Time	Excl Real Time %	Excl Real Time	Calls+RecurCa...	Cpu Time/Call	Real Time/Call
0 (toplevel)	100.0%	1519.207	0.4%	6.334	100.0%	9618.862	0.0%	0.000	11+0	138.110	874.442
1 java/lang/Thread.run ()V	70.0%	1063.654	0.0%	0.034	15.2%	1463.685	0.0%	0.034	1+0	1063.654	1463.685
2 java/util/concurrent/ThreadPoolExecutor$Worker.run ()V	70.0%	1063.620	0.0%	0.027	15.2%	1463.651	0.0%	0.027	1+0	1063.620	1463.651
3 java/util/concurrent/ThreadPoolExecutor.runWorker (Ljava/ut	70.0%	1063.593	0.0%	0.242	15.2%	1463.624	0.0%	0.243	1+0	1063.593	1463.624
4 android/os/AsyncTask$SerialExecutor$1.run ()V	69.8%	1058.792	0.0%	0.082	15.0%	1438.817	0.0%	0.083	1+0	1058.792	1438.817
5 java/util/concurrent/FutureTask.run ()V	69.7%	1058.574	0.0%	0.273	15.0%	1438.599	0.0%	0.100	1+0	1058.574	1438.599
6 android/os/AsyncTask$2.call (Ljava/lang/Object;	69.7%	1058.229	0.0%	0.205	14.6%	1403.016	0.0%	0.205	1+0	1058.229	1403.016
7 com/example/asynctask/MainActivity$1.doInBackground (JL;	69.6%	1056.829	0.0%	0.053	14.4%	1386.631	0.0%	0.054	1+0	1056.829	1386.631
8 com/example/asynctask/MainActivity$1.doInBackground (JL;	69.6%	1056.776	0.0%	0.715	14.4%	1386.577	0.0%	0.734	1+0	1056.776	1386.577
9 android/graphics/BitmapFactory.decodeResource (Landroid;	69.3%	1052.918	0.0%	0.065	14.3%	1377.535	0.0%	0.065	1+0	1052.918	1377.535
10 android/graphics/BitmapFactory.decodeResource (Landroid;	69.3%	1052.853	0.0%	0.224	14.3%	1377.470	0.0%	0.225	1+0	1052.853	1377.470
11 android/graphics/BitmapFactory.decodeResourceStream (La	69.1%	1050.203	0.0%	0.111	14.3%	1374.820	0.0%	0.112	1+0	1050.203	1374.820
12 android/graphics/BitmapFactory.decodeStream (Ljava/io/In	69.1%	1050.040	0.0%	0.164	14.3%	1374.656	0.0%	0.160	1+0	1050.040	1374.656
13 android/graphics/BitmapFactory.nativeDecodeAsset (Landr	69.1%	1049.670	67.0%	1017.229	14.3%	1374.288	10.6%	1017.230	1+0	1049.670	1374.288
14 android/os/Handler.dispatchMessage (Landroid/os/Message	18.8%	286.222	0.0%	0.351	7.0%	673.320	0.0%	0.353	7+0	40.889	96.189
15 android/os/Handler.handleCallback (Landroid/os/Messages;	17.7%	269.202	0.0%	0.271	6.8%	649.073	0.0%	0.275	5+0	53.852	129.815

Find:

On the top is the timeline view, which shows when operations are performed and on which threads they were performed. The methods are each giv-

en a unique color code in the timeline. In order to get a more detailed view in
the timeline, the desired area can be swept out with the mouse.

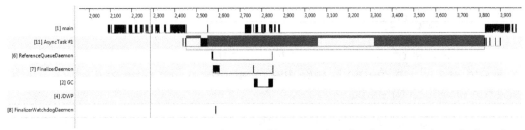

Below the timeline view is the profile panel, which gives detailed information of each method call. There is a wealth of information including how
many times each method was called, both inclusive and exclusive run times
for each method, and other data. Inclusive times are the times that a method
took to execute, including all of the methods that are called within. Exclusive
times only track the time spent performing calculations in that specific method.

8.5.5 Hierarchy View

Open the Hierarchy View in the top right. From here, double click on the Image
Load app's process (in Hierarchy View, the visible process is in bold).

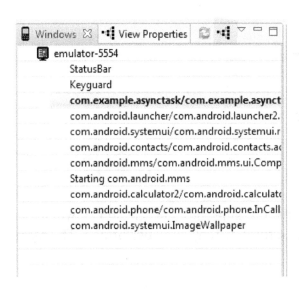

Make sure the *AsyncTask* example process is selected and press the "Load view hierarchy into tree view" button, which is shown above.

The middle view with the tree is the hierarchy of all the *Views* displayed on the screen. Here is a view of the entire application:

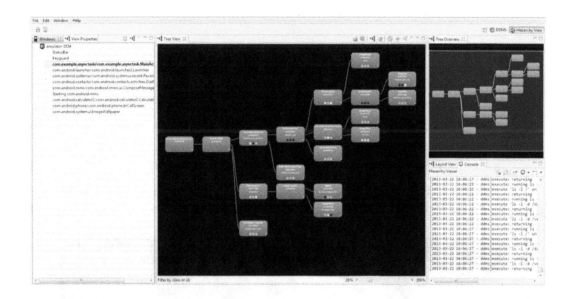

The left-most item in the tree of *View*s is the actual display. To the right is a *LinearLayout* which contains all the parts of the *ActionBar* (the top branch) and the remaining application layout (bottom branch).

The *FrameLayout* is the direct parent of the *ActivityMain.xml* layout, which is simply a *LinearLayout* with a *Button* and *ImageView*. Note that the ID of each *View* is displayed (if the *View* has one).

The three circles at the bottom of each *View* indicate how long different operations took to perform when drawing the *View*. A green circle indicates that

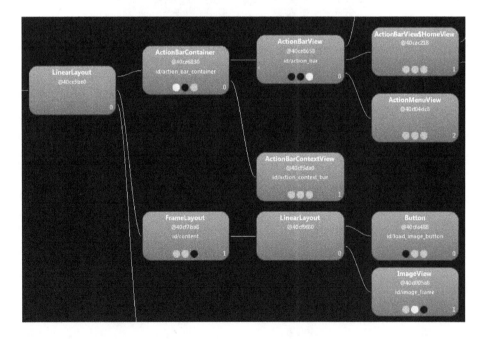

the operation performed more quickly than 50% of all the *Views* in the tree. Yellow means that the operation performed more slowly than 50% of all the *Views* of the tree, and red means that the *View* performed the slowest in its tree.

In any case, the first circle is how long it took for a *View* to be measured. In the simplest of cases, a *View* is defined with dimensions (such as "24dp"); otherwise, the *View* has to either look up or calculate how large it should be. Look ups occur in the cases of *match_parent*, where the parent's dimensions have to be accessed. Calculations occur when *wrap_content* or *layout_weight* are used. In practice, *layout_weight* has the worst performance (especially when a *View* with *layout_weight* is nested inside another *View* with *layout_weight*).

The second circle corresponds to how long the *View* took to "layout". All this step does is determine where to place the *View*.

The final circle is the draw time, which is the actual time it took to draw the *View* on the screen. In this example, the *ImageView* in the application took the longest to draw in its tree. Logically this makes sense because the *ImageView* is drawing a large image.

Clicking the box of a *View* will show the time each operation took to complete.

In the future, if an application has a performance problem, it is a good idea to look at the hierarchy view in order to see which *Views* are taking the longest to be drawn to the screen. This can offer helpful hints on where to look for problems in code.

9 Databases and Animation

9.1 Introduction

At this point now that we have discussed the basic application design techniques, it should be possible to create a usable and useful application. Even still, many common components of applications have not been discussed including preferences (with an associated preference screen), simple database management, and basic animation.

9.2 Preferences

Every good application has some form of a settings screen that allows users to customize small features to their liking. Having a decent set of preferences is often what sets an average apart application from a good application.

Until now, there has not been a way shown to persistently maintain data after an *Activity* has been destroyed. There are multiple means of doing this. The three most common are using Android's built in *PreferenceManager* with *SharedPreferences* using SQLite which is built into Android to create a database (shown in the next section), and writing a file to the file system (not shown in this chapter).

In general, it is a bad idea to write anything but temporary files to the file system where any application can access them. *SharedPreferences* does write its data to the file system, but its files are marked such that they can only be accessed and read by the application that created them. In any case, *SharedPreferences* provides a more secure method of storing data, but sensitive information (such as passwords) should still be encrypted in some way.

SharedPreferences is used in a way similar to *Maps* and *Bundles*. Preferences are stored with a key (of type *String*) in the exact same way as *Bundles*. The only visible difference in the APIs of *Bundle* and *PreferenceManager* is that in order to write a preference, you must use a separate class, *SharedPreferences.Editor*.

The following example makes use of preferences to store the values of *Checkboxes* when a "save" button is pressed and restores the values of the *Checkboxes* when a "restore" button is pressed.

Here is the layout code that simply defines three checkboxes and the two buttons:

```
<LinearLayout xmlns:android="http://schemas.android.com/apk/res/android"
    xmlns:tools="http://schemas.android.com/tools"
    android:layout_width="match_parent"
```

```
android:layout_height="match_parent"
android:orientation="vertical"
android:paddingBottom="@dimen/activity_vertical_margin"
android:paddingLeft="@dimen/activity_horizontal_margin"
android:paddingRight="@dimen/activity_horizontal_margin"
android:paddingTop="@dimen/activity_vertical_margin"
tools:context=".MainActivity" >

<CheckBox
    android:id="@+id/check1"
    android:layout_width="wrap_content"
    android:layout_height="wrap_content"
    android:text="Option 1" />

<CheckBox
    android:id="@+id/check2"
    android:layout_width="wrap_content"
    android:layout_height="wrap_content"
    android:text="Option 2" />

<CheckBox
    android:id="@+id/check3"
    android:layout_width="wrap_content"
    android:layout_height="wrap_content"
    android:text="Option 3" />

<LinearLayout
    android:layout_width="match_parent"
    android:layout_height="0dp"
    android:orientation="horizontal"
    android:layout_weight="1" >

    <Button
        android:id="@+id/load"
        android:layout_width="0dp"
        android:layout_height="wrap_content"
        android:layout_weight="1"
        android:layout_gravity="bottom"
        android:text="Load Settings" />

    <Button
        android:id="@+id/save"
        android:layout_width="0dp"
        android:layout_height="wrap_content"
        android:layout_weight="1"
        android:layout_gravity="bottom"
```

```
                    android:text="Save Settings" />
        </LinearLayout>

</LinearLayout>
```

The Java code:

```java
public class MainActivity extends Activity {
    private Context mContext;
    private SharedPreferences mPrefs;
    private SharedPreferences.Editor mPrefEditor;

    private CheckBox mCheck1;
    private CheckBox mCheck2;
    private CheckBox mCheck3;
    private Button mLoadButton;
    private Button mSaveButton;

    @Override
    protected void onCreate(Bundle savedInstanceState) {
        super.onCreate(savedInstanceState);
        mContext = this;
        setContentView(R.layout.activity_main);

        //Get an instance of the preferences
        mPrefs = PreferenceManager.getDefaultSharedPreferences(mContext);
        mPrefEditor = mPrefs.edit();

        //Find checkboxes
        mCheck1 = (CheckBox) findViewById(R.id.check1);
        mCheck2 = (CheckBox) findViewById(R.id.check2);
        mCheck3 = (CheckBox) findViewById(R.id.check3);

        //Setup Buttons
        mLoadButton = (Button) findViewById(R.id.load);
        mLoadButton.setOnClickListener(new OnClickListener() {
            @Override
            public void onClick(View v) {
                //When "Load" is clicked,
                loadSettings();
            }
        });
```

```
   mSaveButton = (Button) findViewById(R.id.save);
   mSaveButton.setOnClickListener(new OnClickListener() {
      @Override
      public void onClick(View v) {
         //When "Save" is clicked,
         saveSettings();
      }
   });
}
/**
 * Set the checkboxes to
 * what they were last saved as.
 * If nothing was ever saved,
 * all of the checkboxes will not
 * be checked.
 */
private void loadSettings(){
   mCheck1.setChecked(
      mPrefs.getBoolean("check1_checked", false));
   mCheck2.setChecked(
      mPrefs.getBoolean("check2_checked", false));
   mCheck2.setChecked(
      mPrefs.getBoolean("check2_checked", false));
}
/**
 * Save the state  of the checkboxes
 */
private void saveSettings(){
   mPrefEditor.putBoolean("check1_checked",
                  mCheck1.isChecked());
   mPrefEditor.putBoolean("check2_checked",
         mCheck2.isChecked());
   mPrefEditor.putBoolean("check3_checked",
         mCheck3.isChecked());
//write the changes
   mPrefEditor.apply();
   }
}
}
```

SharedPreferences is instantiated by using a static method that takes *Context* as an argument. This method is opening a *File* on the file system that can only be opened by the application with package name as defined in the *Context*.

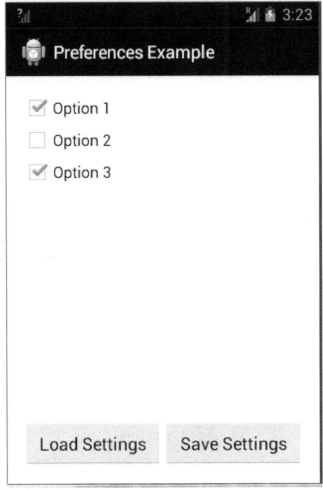

SharedPreferences.Editor also is constructed in an atypical way. The *Editor* is created when the *SharedPreferences* is, so the *edit* method of a *SharedPreferences* object simply returns its associated *Editor*.

In addition to *booleans*, other data types can be put into a *SharedPreferences* file including *floats*, *longs*, *Strings*, and *Set<String>*. Data put into *SharedPrefernces.Editor* will not be saved until *commit* or *apply* is called (which actually writes the data to the file system).

The main difference between *commit* and *apply* is that *commit* returns a *boolean* indicating if the write was successful. Also, *apply* runs asynchronously in a thread. In most cases, it is better to use *apply* so as not to hold back the thread being run (especially if the preference data is being saved on the main thread). In addition to being asynchronous, *apply* typically runs faster because it will not check if writes are successful.

When getting values from *SharedPreference*, two arguments are supplied. The first is simply the key of the item to be retrieved. The second argument is a default value to return if the key does not exist. In this example, if nothing has ever been saved, then the defaults will set all the checkboxes to be unchecked.

Run the example program. Check some of the checkboxes and press "Save Settings," then uncheck/check some of the checkboxes. Pressing "Load settings" now will reset the checkboxes to the state they were in when "Save Settings" was pressed. To prove that preference storage is saved across application restarts, close the application by pressing the "back" button (this will call *finish* and destroy the *Activity*). Open the example program again and press "Load Settings." The checkbox state will be restored.

9.3 PreferenceScreen

One of the biggest advantages of using *SharedPreferences* with *PreferenceManager* is the ability to use the *PreferenceFragment* class, which can easily create detailed preference screens that automatically save changes upon exit.

When using *PreferenceFragment*, all of the preferences can be declared in XML, in a way similar to how declaring layouts in XML works. Then, in a *Prefer-*

enceFragment, the method *addPreferencesFromResources* functions similarly to *setContentView* by inflating the layout from the list of preferences.

There are a few different *Preference* types that can be defined in XML including *CheckBoxPreference*, *EditTextPreference*, and *ListPreference*. The example program uses these three *Preferences*. There are two additional preference types that are not shown here. *SwitchPreference* functions exactly like *CheckBoxPreference*, but visually looks different. *RingtonePreference* functions like a *ListPreference*, except it can allow the user to pick from his or her ringtones and notification sounds.

Preferences can have dependencies. For example, a *Preference* may only be enabled when another preference is. This allows groups of *Preferences* to be "greyed out" (disabled) when a *Preference* is set to *false*. The following example demonstrates this with both "Checkbox Option 1" and "Checkbox Option 2" depending on "Option Editing" being enabled.

Here is a quick look at how the example application functions.

Upon first launch:

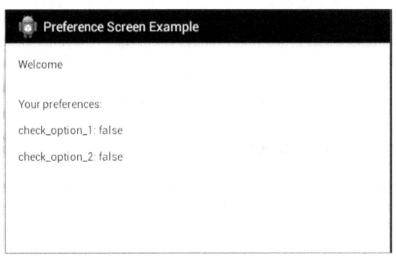

After navigating to settings:

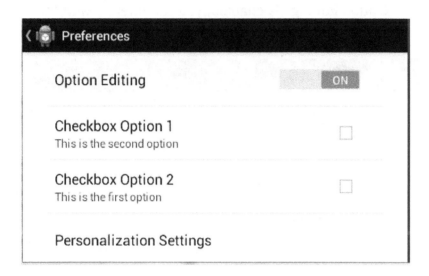

"Checkbox Option 1" and "Checkbox Option 2" are dependent on "Option Editing" being enabled:

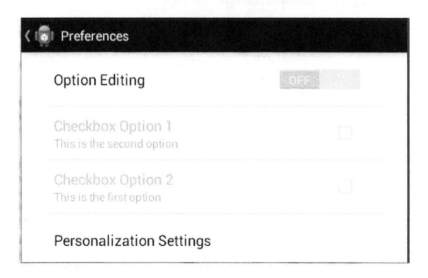

Now that "Option Editing" is enabled, you can interact with the the check-box options.

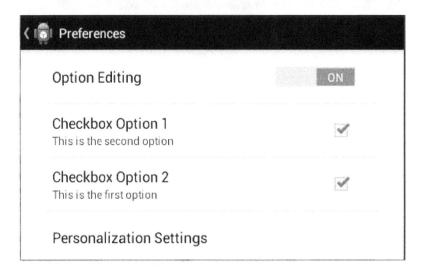

After navigating to "Personalization Settings":

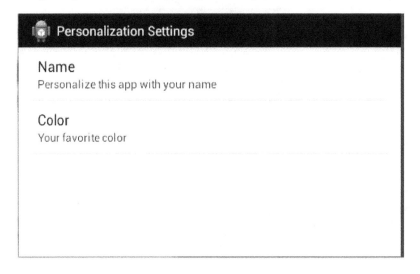

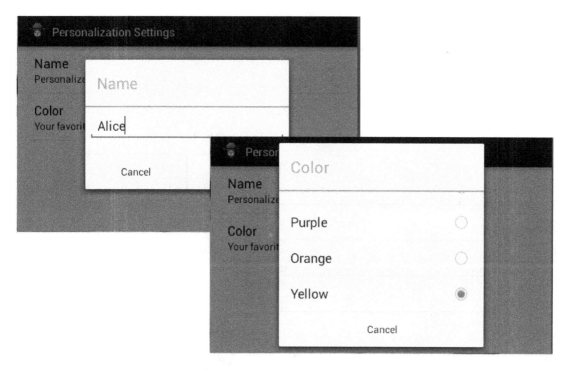

Upon returning to the main screen, the text is updated with the user's preferences:

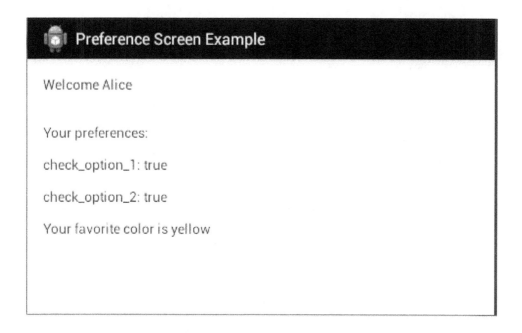

The most interesting source file is the XML definition of the *PreferenceScreen*:

```xml
<?xml version="1.0" encoding="utf-8"?>
<PreferenceScreen
    xmlns:android="http://schemas.android.com/apk/res/android"
    android:key="first_preferencescreen" >

    <SwitchPreference
        android:key="enable_options"
        android:defaultValue="false"
        android:title="Option Editing"/>

    <CheckBoxPreference
        android:key="check_option_1"
        android:dependency="enable_options"
        android:summary="This is the second option"
        android:title="Checkbox Option 1"
        android:defaultValue="false" />
    <CheckBoxPreference
        android:key="check_option_2"
        android:dependency="enable_options"
        android:summary="This is the first option"
        android:title="Checkbox Option 2"
        android:defaultValue="false" />

    <PreferenceScreen
        android:title="Personalization Settings" >
        <EditTextPreference
            android:key="text_name_option"
            android:summary="Personalize this app with your name"
            android:title="Name" />
        <ListPreference
            android:key="text_color_option"
            android:summary="Your favorite color"
            android:title="Color"
            android:entries="@array/colors_array"
            android:entryValues="@array/color_values_array" />
    </PreferenceScreen>

</PreferenceScreen>
```

The root node is a *PreferenceScreen*. *PreferenceScreen* is a means of declaring which options should be grouped together and allow for navigation to deeper levels of options. There always must be a root *PreferenceScreen*. The "Personalization Settings" *PreferenceScreen* is a child of the root *PreferenceScreen*, so it shows as an item. Upon clicking "Personalization Settings," the personalization settings *PreferenceScreen* is shown.

Note that on the *CheckBoxPreferences* that there is an *android:dependency* characteristic. The *dependency* must be a key of a boolean *Preference*. When the *dependency* is false, the dependent preference will be disabled and cannot be interacted with.

ListPreference is the most complicated of the different *Preference* types. *ListPreference* requires two arrays to be declared in XML. *entries* points to an array of *String*s that will be displayed as options. *entryValues* points to an array of *String*s that correspond to each of the items in the *entries* array. *entryValues* will be what is put into the *PreferenceManager*. In this example, the *entries* array contains all of the colors starting with a capital letter. Due to the nature of how the data will be displayed (in a sentence), the *entryValues* simply contains all of the same colors starting with a lower case letter.

Arrays are declared under the *values* folder. If an "arrays.xml" file does not already exist, create it.

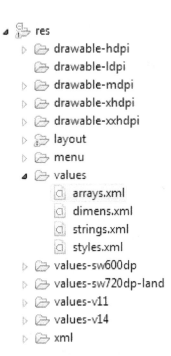

Here is the source of "arrays.xml" that declares the arrays:

```xml
<?xml version="1.0" encoding="utf-8"?>
<resources>
    <string-array name="colors_array">
        <item>Red</item>
        <item>Blue</item>
        <item>Green</item>
        <item>Purple</item>
        <item>Orange</item>
        <item>Yellow</item>
    </string-array>

    <string-array name="color_values_array">
        <item>red</item>
        <item>blue</item>
        <item>green</item>
        <item>purple</item>
```

```
        <item>orange</item>
        <item>yellow</item>
    </string-array>
</resources>
```

This is relatively straightforward. Each *string-array* has a name and a set of *items.*

Here is the method used to automatically inflate layouts from the XML preferences definition:

```java
public class PreferenceActivity extends Activity {

    public static class MyPreferenceFragment extends PreferenceFragment{
        @Override
        public void onCreate(Bundle savedInstanceState){
            super.onCreate(savedInstanceState);
            //Add the preferences from
            //the XML file
            addPreferencesFromResource(R.xml.preferences);
        }
    };

    @Override
    protected void onCreate(Bundle savedInstanceState) {
        super.onCreate(savedInstanceState);
        setContentView(R.layout.activity_preference);

        getActionBar().setDisplayHomeAsUpEnabled(true);

        //If savedInstanceState is not null,
        //then onCreate has already been run once,
        //so there is no need to create a new Fragment
        if(savedInstanceState == null){
            Fragment prefFrag = new MyPreferenceFragment();
            getFragmentManager().beginTransaction()
                        .replace(R.id.preference_fragment_frame,prefFrag)
                        .commit();
        }

    }

    @Override
```

```
   public boolean onOptionsItemSelected(MenuItem item) {
      //If the ActionBar Home button is pressed,
      //leave this Activity
      if(item.getItemId() == android.R.id.home){
         finish();
      }
      return super.onOptionsItemSelected(item);
   }


}
```

PreferenceFragment has its *onCreate* overridden to add preferences from the XML preferences file written. On a side note, the *onCreate* method in *PreferenceActivity* has some interesting logic on when to instantiate and display a new *MyPreferenceFragment*. A *PreferenceFragment* will automatically save its state when the screen is rotated or the *Activity* is paused or stopped. Therefore, when the screen is rotated, the *Activity* should not try to create a new *PreferenceFragment* and replace the old one because this will result in a loss of state.

Finally, the *MainActivity* source:

```
public class MainActivity extends Activity {

   private Context mContext;
   private SharedPreferences mPrefs;
   private TextView mTextView;

   @Override
   protected void onCreate(Bundle savedInstanceState) {
      super.onCreate(savedInstanceState);
      setContentView(R.layout.activity_main);
      mContext = this;
      mPrefs = PreferenceManager.getDefaultSharedPreferences(mContext);
   }

   @Override
   protected void onResume(){
      super.onResume();
```

```
    //Display the text values of all the options
    String textOut = "";

    textOut += "Welcome ";
    textOut += mPrefs.getString("text_name_option", "");

    textOut += "\n\n\nYour preferences:";
    textOut += "\n\ncheck_option_1: ";
    textOut += mPrefs.getBoolean("check_option_1", false);

    textOut += "\n\ncheck_option_2: ";
    textOut += mPrefs.getBoolean("check_option_2", false);

    //If the user setup the color preference,
    //then color will not be an empty String
    String color = mPrefs.getString("text_color_option","");
    if(!color.isEmpty()){
       textOut += "\n\nYour favorite color is " + color;
    }

    mTextView = (TextView) findViewById(R.id.text_output);

    mTextView.setText(textOut);
}

@Override
public boolean onCreateOptionsMenu(Menu menu) {
    // Inflate the menu; this adds items to the action bar if it is
    // present.
    getMenuInflater().inflate(R.menu.main, menu);
    return true;
}

@Override
public boolean onOptionsItemSelected(MenuItem item) {
    //If the "Settings" button is pressed,
    //go to the PreferenceActivity
    if(item.getItemId() == R.id.action_settings){
       Intent i = new Intent(mContext, PreferenceActivity.class);
       startActivity(i);
    }
    return super.onOptionsItemSelected(item);
}

}
```

Preferences declared in an XML file and modified through a *PreferenceFragment* can be read and written to in exactly the same as any other *Preference*, so there is not much to cover in this *Activity*.

9.4 SQLite

Android includes *SQLite*, which can provide in depth, persistent database storage and functionality without much setup. *SQLite* is extremely similar to *SQL*, which is used on the backbends of many web server applications.

When used in a web setting, it is typical to execute *SQL* commands in PHP or some other scripting language. Android has a wrapper class that allows easy access to creating, accessing, reading, and writing to *SQLite* databases.

This sample program will allow users to add small notes (through an *ActionBar* menu item) to a list. It will also allow the user to delete all of the notes.

Here is the application on first startup and when adding a note:

After adding a few notes and after pressing the delete button:

The source for this application is not very complicated, but it does involve writing *SQL* in *Strings*. The Android *SQLiteDatabase* class does have some methods to reduce the amount of *SQL* needed to perform some actions, but these methods tend to be more difficult to understand. This application will write out the *SQL* in *Strings* and make use of *SQLiteDatabase*'s *execSQL* method, which will execute *SQL* code written in a *String*.

For those familiar with *SQL*, the following example is very basic. Even for those without any prior *SQL* experience, the code is very readable.

The bulk of the database management done in this application is in a class called *DatabaseHelper*:

```
public class DatabaseHelper {
   private SQLiteDatabase mDatabase;
   private static final String DATABASENAME = "database1";
   private static final String TABLENAME = "notes";

   public DatabaseHelper(Context context){
      //Open a database with name "database1" that can only be accessed
      //by this application
      mDatabase = context.openOrCreateDatabase(DATABASENAME,
                                   Context.MODE_PRIVATE, null);
      //Open a new table called "notes'
      //"notes" only has one column: a string (varchar) called "Note"
      mDatabase.execSQL("CREATE TABLE IF NOT EXISTS " +
                                   TABLENAME + " (Note VARCHAR);");
   }

   /**
    * Add a note to the table
    * @param noteString The note to be added
    */
   public void addNote(String noteString){
      //Execute SQL that adds a new row
      //where the value of column "Note" is the
      //string passed in
      mDatabase.execSQL("INSERT INTO " + TABLENAME + " (Note)" +
                              " VALUES ('" + noteString + "');");
   }

   /**
    * Deletes the data in the table and creates a new, blank table
    */
   public void delete(){
      //Drop the table used
      mDatabase.execSQL("DROP TABLE IF EXISTS " + TABLENAME);
      //Then create a new blank table
      mDatabase.execSQL("CREATE TABLE IF NOT EXISTS " +
                                   TABLENAME + " (Note VARCHAR);");
   }

   /**
    * @return the notes as an ArrayList of Strings
    */
```

```
public ArrayList<String> generateNoteList() {
   //Create an ArrayList to hold strings
   ArrayList<String> noteList = new ArrayList<String>();

   Cursor c = mDatabase.rawQuery("SELECT * FROM " + TABLENAME, null);
   int noteColumn = c.getColumnIndex("Note");

   if (c.moveToFirst() && c != null) {
      do {
         noteList.add(c.getString(noteColumn));
      } while (c.moveToNext());
   }

   return noteList;
}

}
```

The constructor creates a new *SQLite* database that is *private* (can only be accessed by this application). In *SQL*, databases are comprised of one or more independent tables. This example will only use one table to store the notes.

Both the database and table are given names, which will be used to refer to them later. The table has one column called *Note* which accepts the data type *VARCHAR* (*String*s and character arrays are equivalent to *SQL*'s *VARCHAR* data type).

The *addNote* method uses the *SQL INSERT* command to insert a *String* into the column *Note*. The syntax of *SQL* may look strange to a beginner. This chapter will not be teaching *SQL* in depth, but rather showing how to use *SQL* in Android. *www.sqlite.org* contains a full set of documentation on *SQLite*, and there are a myriad of online *SQL* learning tools available.

The *delete* method drops the table (effectively deleting it) and creates a new blank table of the same name.

Finally, the *generateNoteList* method is what the *Activity* will use to populate an *ArrayAdapter* for a *ListView*. *generateNoteList* uses a *Cursor*. *Cursor*s are able to navigate through a table, sort the table, and perform basic searches. This

Cursor selects all of the rows (because it uses *, the wildcard character, which indicates that any row should be selected). After selecting rows, the *Cursor* can navigate through them.

First, the column(s) have to be found. Each column is given an id. Here, the *int noteColumn* stores the index of the column *Note*. Then, a *do while* loop is used to navigate through the selected rows. This code uses an *if* statement to make sure that the cursor is not null and that the cursor was able to move to the first row selected. *moveToFirst* will return false only if there are no rows selected. The *Strings* in each row in the *Note* column are added to the *ArrayList* and eventually returned.

The layout is simply a *ListView*, so the code is not shown here.

The menu XML file has two options, an add note option and a delete option. Note that the strings and drawables used here have been added to the project.

```
<menu xmlns:android="http://schemas.android.com/apk/res/android" >
    <item
        android:id="@+id/action_add"
        android:icon="@drawable/ic_action_new"
        android:orderInCategory="1"
        android:showAsAction="always"
        android:title="@string/action_add"/>
    <item
        android:id="@+id/action_delete"
        android:icon="@drawable/ic_action_delete"
        android:orderInCategory="2"
        android:showAsAction="ifRoom"
        android:title="@string/delete"/>
</menu>
```

Finally, here is the code for the *Activity*:

```
public class MainActivity extends Activity {
    ListView mList;
    DatabaseHelper mDbHelper;
```

```java
    @Override
    protected void onCreate(Bundle savedInstanceState) {
        super.onCreate(savedInstanceState);
        setContentView(R.layout.activity_main);

        mList = (ListView) findViewById(R.id.list);

        // Instantiate the database
        mDbHelper = new DatabaseHelper(this);

        // Show the notes
        updateList();
    }

    /**
     * Gets the notes from the SQLite database and displays them in the
ListView
     */
    public void updateList() {
        // Get an ArrayList of the notes
        ArrayList<String> noteList = mDbHelper.generateNoteList();
        // Generate an ArrayAdapter with the notes
        ArrayAdapter<String> adapter = new ArrayAdapter<String>(this,
            android.R.layout.simple_list_item_1, noteList);
        // Set the ListView's adapter
        mList.setAdapter(adapter);
    }

    public void addNoteDialog() {
        // New note dialog
        AlertDialog diag = new AlertDialog.Builder(this).create();
        diag.setTitle(getString(R.string.add_title));

        // Edit Text to allow text input
        final EditText noteInput = new EditText(this);
        noteInput.setHint(getString(R.string.note));

        // Set the dialog view to show the EditText
        diag.setView(noteInput);

        diag.setButton(DialogInterface.BUTTON_NEGATIVE,
            getString(R.string.cancel),
            new DialogInterface.OnClickListener() {
                @Override
                public void onClick(DialogInterface dialog, int which) {
                    // Do nothing on "Cancel" press,
```

```
                    // The dialog will automatically close
            }
        });

    diag.setButton(DialogInterface.BUTTON_POSITIVE,
        getString(R.string.add), new DialogInterface.OnClickListener(){
            @Override
            public void onClick(DialogInterface dialog, int which) {
                // Create a note with the text
                String text = noteInput.getText().toString();
                // Check to make sure the user entered text
                if (!text.isEmpty()) {
                        mDbHelper.addNote(text);
                        updateList();
                }
            }
        });

    diag.show();
}

@Override
public boolean onCreateOptionsMenu(Menu menu) {
    // Inflate the menu; this adds items to the action bar if it is
    // present.
    getMenuInflater().inflate(R.menu.main, menu);
    return true;
}

@Override
public boolean onOptionsItemSelected(MenuItem item) {
    switch (item.getItemId()) {
    case R.id.action_add:
        // Add note option
        addNoteDialog();
        break;
    case R.id.action_delete:
        // Delete table action
        mDbHelper.delete();
        // After deleting and recreating
        // the table, update the ListView
        // to show the changes
        updateList();
        break;
    }
    return super.onOptionsItemSelected(item);
```

```
    }

}
```

This code is self-explanatory now that the *DatabaseHelper* class has been explained. The code in the *addNoteDialog* method is very similar to code used in a sample when *Dialog* boxes were first introduced, and the *updateList* code is simply using an *ArrayAdapter* to populate a *ListView*.

This application does nothing when a note is pressed, but it would not be difficult to add that functionality (simply set an *OnItemClickListener*, which has been demonstrated before).

9.5 Animation

Animations are a great way to add extra polish to an interface. Animations should be used sparingly. Too many (or too long) animations will appear glitzy, but a few key transitions can highlight functionality and make an application a joy to use.

This example demonstrates how to show and hide *CheckBoxes* upon the press of a button, but the methods used will work with any *View*.

This demonstration of *Animations* uses *ViewPropertyAnimator*, which was introduced in Android version 3.1. In previous versions of Android, using animations followed the same general process, but involved more boilerplate and was more difficult for developers to use.

In order to begin animating a view, simply call *animate* which returns a *ViewPropertyAnimator*. The *ViewPropertyAnimator* can be set to change any characteristic of a *View* including scale, size, rotation, alpha (transparency), and translation. The duration of the animation and a start delay can be specified as well.

Once setting all of these characteristics, calling *start* will begin the animation.

Here is the XML layout that is used:

```
<RelativeLayout
xmlns:android="http://schemas.android.com/apk/res/android"
    xmlns:tools="http://schemas.android.com/tools"
    android:layout_width="match_parent"
    android:layout_height="match_parent"
    android:orientation="vertical"
    tools:context=".MainActivity" >

    <CheckBox
        android:id="@+id/choice1"
        android:layout_width="wrap_content"
        android:layout_height="wrap_content"
        android:layout_alignParentLeft="true"
        android:layout_alignParentTop="true"
        android:layout_marginLeft="8dp"
        android:layout_marginTop="8dp"
        android:text="Choice 1" />

    <CheckBox
        android:id="@+id/choice2"
        android:layout_width="wrap_content"
        android:layout_height="wrap_content"
        android:layout_alignParentLeft="true"
        android:layout_below="@id/choice1"
        android:layout_marginLeft="8dp"
        android:text="Choice 2" />

    <CheckBox
        android:id="@+id/extra_choice3"
        android:layout_width="wrap_content"
        android:layout_height="wrap_content"
        android:layout_alignParentLeft="true"
        android:layout_below="@id/choice2"
        android:layout_marginLeft="8dp"
        android:alpha="0"
        android:text="Extra choice 3" />

    <CheckBox
        android:id="@+id/extra_choice4"
        android:layout_width="wrap_content"
```

```
          android:layout_height="wrap_content"
          android:layout_alignParentLeft="true"
          android:layout_below="@id/extra_choice3"
          android:layout_marginLeft="8dp"
          android:alpha="0"
          android:text="Extra choice 4" />

   <Button
          android:id="@+id/more_choices"
          android:layout_width="wrap_content"
          android:layout_height="wrap_content"
          android:layout_alignParentBottom="true"
          android:layout_centerHorizontal="true"
          android:layout_marginBottom="8dp"
          android:text="Show Extra Choices" />

</RelativeLayout>
```

The only special parts of this layout are the third and fourth checkboxes. These checkboxes should be hidden by default, so their alpha (transparency) is set to o. Alpha is expressed as a percentage, so o is completely transparent and 1 is completely opaque.

The Java code below animates the checkboxes in and out when the button is pressed and also restores state after pauses or stops.

```
public class MainActivity extends Activity {
   private CheckBox mCheck1;
   private CheckBox mCheck2;
   private CheckBox mCheck3;
   private CheckBox mCheck4;
   private Button mMoreButton;
   private boolean mExtrasShown = false;

   @Override
   protected void onCreate(Bundle savedInstanceState) {
      super.onCreate(savedInstanceState);
      setContentView(R.layout.activity_main);

      getActionBar().setTitle("Animation Example");

      //Find the important Views
```

```
mCheck1 = (CheckBox) findViewById(R.id.choice1);
mCheck2 = (CheckBox) findViewById(R.id.choice2);
mCheck3 = (CheckBox) findViewById(R.id.extra_choice3);
mCheck4 = (CheckBox) findViewById(R.id.extra_choice4);
mMoreButton = (Button) findViewById(R.id.more_choices);

mMoreButton.setOnClickListener(new OnClickListener() {
    @Override
    public void onClick(View v) {
        //Check if the extra options are
        //already shown
        if(mExtrasShown){
            //The extra options should be hidden
            slideOutOptions();
        }else{
            //The extra options should be shown
            slideInOptions();
        }

        //Change the state of whether or not the
        //extra checkboxes are shown
        mExtrasShown = !mExtrasShown;
    }
});

//Restore state from
if(savedInstanceState != null){
    restoreCheckboxes(savedInstanceState);
}
}

@Override
protected void onSaveInstanceState(Bundle outState) {
    super.onSaveInstanceState(outState);
    outState.putBoolean("check1", mCheck1.isChecked());
    outState.putBoolean("check2", mCheck2.isChecked());
    outState.putBoolean("check3", mCheck3.isChecked());
    outState.putBoolean("check4", mCheck4.isChecked());
    outState.putBoolean("extras_shown", mExtrasShown);
}

/**
 * Restores the checkbox state over pauses and stops
 * @param savedInstanceState Bundle of saved instance state
 */
private void restoreCheckboxes(Bundle savedInstanceState){
```

```java
    boolean check1 = false;
    boolean check2 = false;
    boolean check3 = false;
    boolean check4 = false;

    if(savedInstanceState.containsKey("check1")){
       check1 = savedInstanceState.getBoolean("check1");
    }
    if(savedInstanceState.containsKey("check2")){
       check2 = savedInstanceState.getBoolean("check2");
    }
    if(savedInstanceState.containsKey("check3")){
       check3 = savedInstanceState.getBoolean("check3");
    }
    if(savedInstanceState.containsKey("check4")){
       check4 = savedInstanceState.getBoolean("check4");
    }

    mCheck1.setChecked(check1);
    mCheck2.setChecked(check2);
    mCheck3.setChecked(check3);
    mCheck4.setChecked(check4);

    if(savedInstanceState.containsKey("extras_shown")){
       if(savedInstanceState.getBoolean("extras_shown")){
          mExtrasShown = true;
          slideInOptions();
       }
    }
 }


/**
 * Show the extra options
 */
private void slideInOptions(){
   mMoreButton.setText("Hide Extra Choices");

   //Translate the checkboxes 100 pixels left
   mCheck3.setX(-100);
   mCheck4.setX(-100);

   //Animate to being opaque and
   //slide in checkboxes
   //delay the second checkbox animation
   //75 milliseconds for extra effect
```

```
      mCheck3.animate()
          .alpha(1f)
          .translationX(0)
          .setDuration(250)
          .start();
    mCheck4.animate()
          .alpha(1f)
          .translationX(0)
          .setDuration(250)
          .setStartDelay(75)
          .start();
  }

  /**
   * Hide the extra options
   */
  public void slideOutOptions(){
    mMoreButton.setText("Show Extra Choices");

    //Slide out animation,
    //animated to being transparent and
    //slide 100 pixels left
    mCheck3.animate()
          .alpha(0f)
          .translationX(-100)
          .setDuration(250)
          .start();
    mCheck4.animate()
          .alpha(0f)
          .translationX(-100)
          .setDuration(250)
          .setStartDelay(75)
          .start();
  }

}
```

slideInOptions is the method used to make the extra checkboxes opaque and slide them in from the left. In order to slide them from the left, they first must be moved to the left. This is accomplished through the *setX* method, which is available on every *View*. Then the animation can occur. First *animate* is called to get a *ViewPropertyAnimator*. From there, the characteristics to be animated to are set. Then duration of the animation is set (in milliseconds). If *setDuration* is never called, then a default of 300 milliseconds will be used. This example code uses *setStartDelay* on the fourth *CheckBox* for added effect by delaying the start of the fourth *CheckBox*. Finally, *start* is called and the animation begins.

As for other features in this code, *onSaveInstanceState* and *restoreCheckboxes* save and restore the *CheckBoxes* state (including whether or not the extra checkboxes are shown).

This is a good use case for an animation. Animations are best used when something on the screen changes because of user interaction. Avoid needless or excessive animations. Avoid using animations longer than 500 milliseconds. A good interface will have subtle animations that add polish but do not hinder or slow down users.

10 Creating a Commercial App

10.1 Introduction

Now that the application design techniques have been discussed and used individually, it is time to bring all of the skills together and create a full-fledged application. This chapter seeks to assist in developing an entire application that uses preferences, restores state, has interesting layouts, uses subtle animations, is designed for good performance, has dialogs, and keeps persistent storage of data.

This chapter will also cover one of the most overlooked parts of application design: iconography. Icons are perhaps one of the most important parts of an application, especially the "launcher icon" used on the store listing and the home screen. Icons are also used in the *ActionBar* and can be interspersed anywhere in an application.

Finally, this chapter will explain how to create an Android installable package (.apk file) and demonstrates the process of publishing an application on Google Play.

10.2 Iconography

The first part of any application that a user will see is the icon. If an application's main icon looks unprofessional, it makes no difference how useful or good looking the application is. When browsing applications to install, most users simply search for what they want and then scroll through lists of application with their icons and titles. If neither the icon nor the title is appealing, it is highly unlikely that a potential user will tap to see more details.

10.2.1 Tools

To design icons, you will need a fully featured image editor or drawing application. Many designers work with Adobe Photoshop or other professional software. For the purposes of only designing an icon, free software like Gimp or Inkscape will do. This book will use Gimp, which is available on **www.gimp.org**

Do not be inclined to use tools like Paint (bundled with Windows). These tools are too basic and do not have support for some of the features needed to make a proper icon.

10.2.2 Launcher Icons

The launcher icon is the most critical of the icons. It will have a significant effect on how many people download an application. Launcher icons should have a slight three dimensional effect, as if they were viewed from above. Here is an example.

Instead of using a two dimensional box like this:

Use a pseudo three dimensional box:

Of course, this is a very simple example and a very boring shape, but it illustrates the concept.

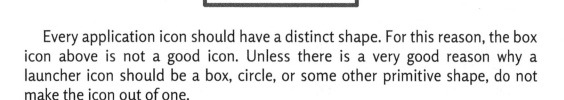

Every application icon should have a distinct shape. For this reason, the box icon above is not a good icon. Unless there is a very good reason why a launcher icon should be a box, circle, or some other primitive shape, do not make the icon out of one.

Here is an example of a distinct shape:

This is the stock open-source Android launcher icon for the Camera application. Note the distinct shape of the outline of the icon. The lens goes past the bottom of the rectangular camera body, making the silhouette unique. Also, the shutter button protrudes from the top, as well as the viewfinder. The abnormal shape gives the icon a three dimensional feeling.

Another technique that this icon uses to further increase the three dimensional feeling is the use of lighting. Surfaces that are on the top of the camera are very light, and surfaces underneath edges receive a soft shadow effect.

Once all of the above effects are combined, the final product looks fantastic and fits in with the rest of the launcher icons.

10.2.3 Designing a Launcher Icon

Start by drawing the icon large and then resize the icon later. It is a good idea to draw the icon at 1024 by 1024 pixels or even larger. The icon used for display in the Google Play store is 512 by 512 pixels, but it is always easier to downsize an icon than to upsize it later, which will result in a loss of sharpness and detail.

Begin by creating an outline of the icon. It is always a good idea to make rough sketches of the design by hand. The outline should fill the entire canvas (there should be little or no white space around the edges. If there is, it is not a big problem, as the resizing tool used later will automatically eliminate the white space.

Next fill in the outline. If the fill will be a solid color, it typically looks best to use a radial gradient with a slightly lighter and a slightly darker shade of the color desired. This results in a slight glow effect darker at the edges and brighter in the middle. Depending on what tool is used, the process of creating a radial gradient fill will wildly differ.

Next add details to the icon. Adding too little detail will result in a boring icon, but adding too much detail may result in the icon looking cluttered and out of place. Try to find the balance between the two. It always helps to look at other icons of applications in the Google Play store.

Finally add subtle lighting and shadow effects. Be careful not to overdo the effect. There are many different ways to create shadows, but the most common would be to use a brush with a dark grey color and about 50% opacity. Then simply brush wherever shadows should be. Lighting is accomplished in a similar way, but uses white instead of grey. It will take some experimentation to get the opacity and color correct.

In practice, icon design can take anywhere from a few hours to days. Often times the first versions of the icon will look flawed, but after a few revisions icons tend to reach their final forms. Not all icons have to be as complicated as the Android camera icon is. All an icon has to do is communicate what the application does.

Now that the icon is made at a high resolution, it is time to resize it for the different screen densities. This can be done in any decent photo editor, but the ADT plugin has a tool to resize icons to the correct resolutions and will place each of those in the correct *drawable* folder.

In Eclipse, navigate to *File*, then *New*, then *Other...* and finally *Android Icon Set*, which is located under the *Android* heading. Choose what kind of icon is being created (in this case a launcher icon), the project to insert this icon into, and then give the icon a name.

Here is the screen that allows icons to be resized. Placeholder icons can be made from clipart or text. This example is using an already made icon that only needs to be resized, so press *Image* and browse to the icon image file that has been created.

The Android Asset studio allows a three dimensional square or circle background to be added to an icon. Ideally, the three dimensional perspective would already be done (because squares and circles are boring shapes).

This sample icon has very little three dimensionality, so the square background will be applied.

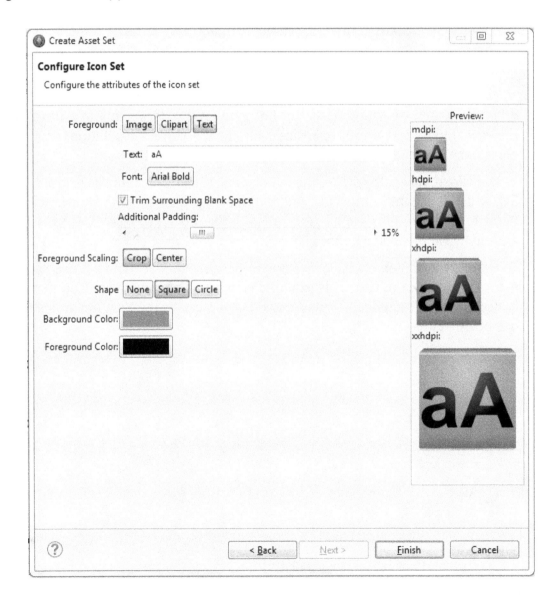

After applying the square background, this icon looks more respectable and fitting for an Android application.

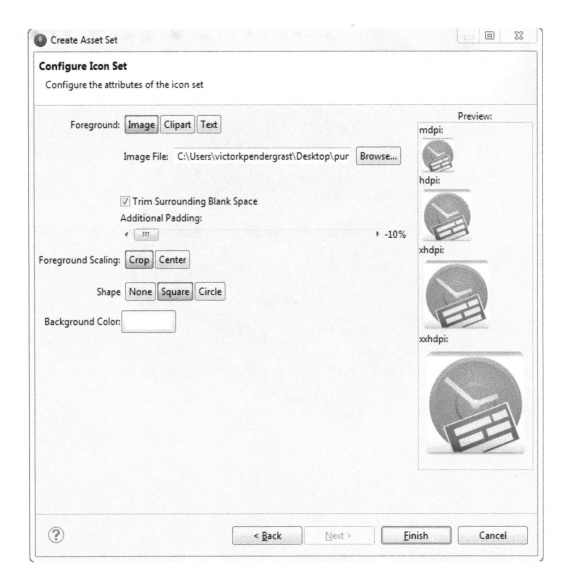

Pressing finish will put all of the resized icons into the previously selected project. Run whatever project this icon set was put into and the launcher icon will have changed from the default one.

If the launcher icon did not change, you may change the drawable re-source used for the launcher icon in the manifest.

Here is the icon after adding the square background and the icon used in the animation sample application:

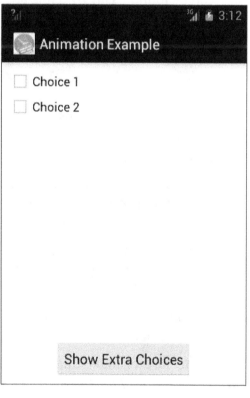

10.2.4 **ActionBar Icons**

Icons made for the ActionBar are significantly simpler. They are a solid color and are flat. ActionBar Icons do not use fancy lighting or three dimensional effects.

A number of ActionBar icons are included in the *Action Bar Icon Pack*, which is available for download in the developer section of the Android website. It can be found easily by using any search engine.

Here are a few examples from the *Action Bar Icon Pack*:

Although these icons are significantly simpler, they can be more difficult to design. It can be a tedious process to create a small monotone icon that clearly communicates an action.

Fortunately, all the common icons you will need are already available in the *Action Bar Icon Pack*. In the event that the pack does not contain a specific icon that you would like to use, here are the basic steps to create one:

Start with a smaller canvas than when designing launcher icons. 256 by 256 is a good size. The background should be completely transparent, as it was with the launcher icon design.

You may design in any color, because the icon set creation tool in Eclipse will automatically recolor the non-transparent areas.

Be sure to make lines thick and avoid adding too much detail. ActionBar Icons are very small when displayed in an app, so too much detail will only make the icon look grainy.

Here is an example of a raw clipboard/note icon:

Here is the icon imported in the icon set creation tool:

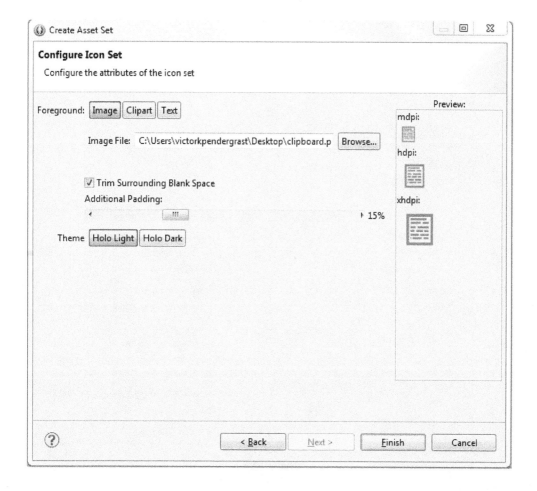

Now the icon can be used in the ActionBar by editing a menu XML file to include a *MenuItem* with an icon referring to that drawable.

10.3 Exporting an Application

With the icons created and the application developed, it is time to export the application so it can be installed on devices (and published to Google Play).

Android applications are delivered as .apk files. In order to create one, simply right click on a project in Eclipse. Go to *Android Tools*, and then click

Export Signed Application Package...

If this is the first time you are creating a .apk file, a new keystore file will have to be created. Keystore files are used to validate developers. If a user tries to update an application with a .apk file signed with a different keystore, the system will not allow it. This is a means of adding security to Android.

Create a new keystore by designating where it should be saved and give it a password:

Now you will need to create an alias. Keystores allow for multiple aliases (for when multiple developers are working on a project). Create an alias with a password and fill out the information asked for. Note that the Validity (years) field is recommended to be at least thirty years.

Finally, browse to where the .apk file should be saved and click *Finish*:

Now this .apk file can be downloaded on an Android device (as an email attachment or from a website) and installed. It can also be uploaded to Google Play.

10.4 Publishing to Google Play

Google Play is the biggest app market for Android. The process for publishing an application to Google Play changes often, but is straightforward.

The first step in publishing an application is to create a developer account. This can be done at *www.play.google.com/apps/publish*

Click "Sign Up" and fill out the requested information. You will have to pay a one-time, $25 fee for creating a publisher account. Once your account is set-up, you will be able to upload an app.

The developer console interface changes periodically, so the following process may change slightly. First create a new application in the developer console by clicking "Add New Application."

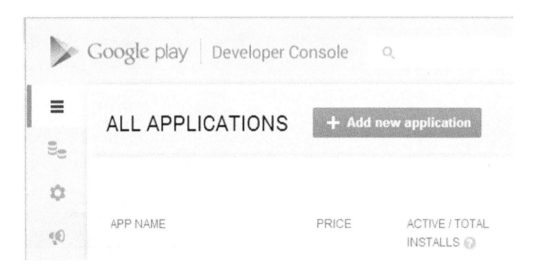

Write a title for your application. The next step is to either upload the .apk file or prepare the store listing (description, screenshots, etc.). Each step can be completed independently.

Uploading a .apk is a very straightforward process that involves browsing to the file's location and selecting it.

As for the store listing, first write a description. Descriptions should be short and to the point. Describe what the application does and what makes it unique. It is a good idea to propose a typical use case for the application. For example, a note taking application may be used to write down shopping lists for later use. Finally, descriptions should have a call to action. Usually this is one sentence telling potential customers why it is a good idea to install the application. Example for a note taking application: "Download *app_name* and you'll always remember what matters most!"

Next, fill out the promo text. This field is optional, but it will help users discover the application. This is a short sentence describing what the app does.

The next field, "Recent Changes" is used to tell users what is new in an update. This will be explained further shortly.

Now upload screenshots. On Android devices running Android 3.0 and higher, there is a key combination to take a screenshot and save it to the device. Usually, the combination involves holding the power button and the volume down button, but on some Samsung devices, the combination is the power button and the home button.

Once the screenshots are saved, transfer them to a computer either through email or USB.

If you only have access to an emulator, take a screenshot of the desktop and use an image editor (like Gimp) to crop the image to only the emulator's screen.

The developer console requires at least two screenshots. A new addition to the developer console is the ability to publish separate screenshots for tablets and phones. When a user is browsing the store, the appropriate set of screenshots will be shown.

Next, upload a high resolution (512 by 512 pixels) version of the application icon.

The feature graphic and promo graphic are optional, but highly recommended. There are no real guidelines to these two graphics so they come in all different styles. It is a good idea to browse the apps section of *play.google.com* to get ideas.

A YouTube promo video may also be linked to and displayed alongside the screenshots. When creating a video, keep it shorter than two minutes and highlight the unique features of the application.

Select a category for the application and the age group this app appeals to.

Fill out the pricing of the application on the "Pricing and Distribution" page. Note that if the application is published as free, it will never be allowed to be published with a price.

Select which countries the app will be published in. This can be changed at any time.

Read and accept the Content Guidelines and the US export laws.

At this point, pressing "Publish" will publish the application the market. It may take a few hours until it becomes available.

In order to release an update for an application, the app's version and version code (declared in the manifest) has to be incremented.

```
<?xml version="1.0" encoding="utf-8"?>
<manifest xmlns:android="http://schemas.android.com/apk/res/android"
    package="com.example.animations"
    android:versionCode="1"
    android:versionName="1.0" >
```

Then simply upload a new .apk through the developer console. It is always a good idea to add details to the "Recent Changes" indicating what the new update adds or fixes.

10.5 Suggested Applications

One of the most common applications that new developers make is a notepad app with basic functionality (creating notes, editing notes, and deleting notes). It is typical to store the notes in an SQL database.

Previews of the note (only the first few words) are displayed in a list on the main screen (on tablets, the list is displayed in a fragment on the left). Upon clicking a note preview, the full note is displayed. From there, it can be edited or deleted.

Try adding extra polish to the application by designing interesting layouts and by using attention-grabbing animations. It might be a good idea to start with the SQL Note example and adapt it to use *Fragments* (for listing the notes and displaying the notes in their entirety). As for the individual note delete functionality, the *SQL* command *DELETE* can be used.

10.6 Final Thoughts

There are still many more topics that this book did not cover, primarily because of their reliance on third parties. These topics include how to add advertisements to an application (which is commonly done with AdMob), in-app purchases (which vary based on which store the application is being distributed through), and some of the more notable third party libraries (such as Google Maps and ZXing, which allows any application to scan barcodes).

Some other notable topics that haven't been covered include notifications and creating services. Both of these are straightforward. *Services* are written similarly to *Activities*, and notifications are rather basic to learn.

Now that you have a good foundation and understanding of Android, the developer documentation available on *developer.android.com* should be able to guide you through topics that were not taught in this book.

This book also did not go in depth on networking partly because it is exactly the same as it is in standard Java, but also because most applications do not need it. Applications that do use networking extensively typically have a server backend that would add enough complexity to be the subject of a standalone book.

The Android developer community is relatively mature when compared to other mobile platforms, so there are many tutorials and examples available online. If at any point some information is not already available online, consider asking a question or searching for answers on www.stackoverflow.com, which is question and answer community for software deveolopers.

Congratulations on completing this book and good luck creating Android apps!

INDEX